EUROPEAN HOURS
COLLECTED POEMS

Anthony Rudolf was born in 1942 in London, where he still lives. He has two children and three grandchildren. He studied modern languages and social anthropology at Trinity College, Cambridge. He is a major translator of literary works from French, Russian and other languages: these include books by Yves Bonnefoy, Claude Vigée, Edmond Jabès and Evgeny Vinokurov. He is also the author of a trilogy of memoirs: *Silent Conversations: a Reader's Life*, *A Vanished Hand* and *The Arithmetic of Memory*. His critical work includes the first extended study in English of Primo Levi and a wide range of essays on international modernist writers – among them F.T. Prince, Piotr Rawicz and George Oppen – and artists such as Kitaj and Hammershøi. He was the founder and publisher of Menard Press. A former Visiting Lecturer in Arts and Humanities at London Metropolitan University, he is Fellow of the Royal Society of Literature and the English Association, and Chevalier de l'ordre des Arts et des Lettres. In 1998, under the narrative influence of Paula Rego, he turned to fiction, completing a book of prose fables.

Anthony Rudolf's publications include

Poetry
The Same River Twice
After the Dream
Zigzag: Five Verse/Prose Sequences

Memoirs
The Arithmetic of Memory
Silent Conversations: A Reader's Life
A Vanished Hand: My Autograph Album

Fiction
Kafka's Doll

Criticism
At an Uncertain Hour: Primo Levi's War against Oblivion
Wine from Two Glasses: Poetry and Politics
Jerzyk: Diaries, Texts and Testimonies
Engraved in Flesh: Piotr Rawicz and Blood from the Sky

Book Translations
French Poetry: Yves Bonnefoy, Edmond Jabès, Claude Vigée
Russian Poetry: Alexander Tvardovsky, Evgeny Vinokurov
Other Poetry: Miriam Neiger-Fleischmann, lfigenija Simonovic
Drama and fiction etc.: Balzac, Jean Clair,
Eugene Heimler, Ana Novac

ANTHONY RUDOLF

EUROPEAN HOURS
COLLECTED POEMS

CARCANET

First published in Great Britain in 2017 by
Carcanet Press Limited
Alliance House, 30 Cross Street,
Manchester, M2 7AQ
www.carcanet.co.uk

A CIP catalogue record for this book is
available from the British Library,
ISBN 978 1 784102 08 1

Typeset in Great Britain by XL Publishing, Exmouth, Devon

The publisher acknowledges financial
assistance from Arts Council England.

Supported by
ARTS COUNCIL
ENGLAND

Dedicated to Paula Rego
at home, in the studio, in Europe

Contents

PROLOGUE

European Hours   3

I.   1964–1971

Tree	11
Stones	11
The Waves	12
The Grave	12
Obsession: A Structure	13
Land of Ancient Moons	14
Heater	15
Necessary Fiction	16
East Sixth Street, 1966	16
The Sound of the Land: Reflection	17
Childhood	19
Dimension	20
Blackheath: Autumn	20
To a Voice	21
Beach	21
For All We Know	22
Structure of Feeling	24
The Reflection	25
Return to Ashkelon	26
Manifold Circle	28

Invisible Ink	29
Pebble	30
Picture on the Wall: No-Man's-Landscape	31
Lucien Stryk	32
Evening of the Rose	33
Checkpoint Charlie	34
6.30 p.m. On the Dot	35

II. 1972–1976

Twelve Fragments	
Early Photograph of Michael Hamburger	39
Primrose Gardens, London NW3	39
Sister of the Sea	39
Onion	40
Grandmother	40
Mother Tongue	40
In Memoriam	41
Recollection	41
Joseph Rudolf, 92, Speaks to his Grandson	41
Matisse Chapel, Vence	42
Careless Love	42
The Lost Tribe	42
Late Night	43
England	43
Song Recital in a City Church	45
'Tout lecteur est l'élu d'un livre'	45
Reveille	47
Dubrovnik Poem	47
A Presence	49
Empty Houses	50
The Translator Addresses Borges	50
Dream Time	51
Kensington Palace Gardens	52
Saint-Paul de Vence	53

Chez Maeght (Saint-Paul de Vence)	54
Chagall	55
Balthus	56
Three Poems of the Grave	
Power Cut	57
In his Death	58
Kafka's Tomb	58
Prayer for Kafka and Ourselves	59
Amsterdam	59
A History of Silence	60
Edward Hopper	61
Z. Kotowicz Reading Bachelard on a Train	62
The Same River Twice	62
Redemption Song	63
Last Poem of Karl Kraus (1936)	64
Emma Van Name	64

III.   1977–1991

Ancient of Days	67
Against Anxiety	68
'The True Inflections...'	69
Picture at an Exhibition	70
Invocations for a Work in Clay	71
Autumnal	71
Ancient Beams	72
Halfway through Life	73
Parmerde Junphe 1872	74
Catalogue Sonnet	75
Old Man	76
Process Verbal	77
Reading Stevens in Hospital	77
Vasko Popa in Cambridge	78
In Memoriam	78
Et in Arcadia Ego	79

Noonday   80
Headland   81
Breughel to Auden   82
Poem-em   82

IV   1992–2013

Antique Land   87
You, Painting   88
Fran Sinclair   89
Bonnard: the Last Picture   90
In Memoriam Gisèle Celan-Lestrange   91
Colombine at the Picasso Exhibition, Paris, November 1996   92
Branca's Vineyard   93
'The Bread of Faithful Speech'   94
Removal Man   97
Circle of Knowledge   98
Architexture   99
Rider on the Rocking Horse   101
'Damasio Abstracted'   102
Final Proof   103
Unter den Linden   104
Found Poem   105
Two Linked Poems for Charlie
    1) Dunedin: Botanical Gardens   107
    2) Wellington: Queen's Wharf   108
Your Mind Surprises Itself   109
Pillar Box, Well Walk NW3   110

V   Two Long Poems

Mandorla   113
Zigzag (Teaching Autobiography, 2000–2003)   119

VI   Proses

The Second Oldest Poet   135

Text for Jane Bustin   136
Vilhelm Hammershøi   137
Notebook   139
A Coherent Deformation: Arturo Di Stefano   142
Screen Memory   145
Yves Bonnefoy: The Re-invention of Death (One)   146
Jerzyk: The Reinvention of Death (Two)   146

Notes   149
Appendix
    Old Wyldes   159
Acknowledgments   163

Index of Titles   165
Index of First Lines   169

PROLOGUE

EUROPEAN HOURS
(INVOCATIONS)

To ancestral Europe: your Iberia, my Austria-Hungary. (To London…)

★★

(Lisbon)
To your *azulejos* tiles, commissioned by the Marquis of Fronteira for the garden of his Palacio.

To 'Saint Vincent's Panels' by Nuno Gonçalves and Bosch's triptych 'The Temptation of Saint Anthony' in the Museu Nacional de Arte Antiga.

To your paintings in the chapel of the President's palace at Belém (and to a house of stories twenty miles away).

★★

(London)
To Piero di Cosimo's 'Battle between the Lapiths and the Centaurs' in the National Gallery, a favourite picture you always study closely.

To your studio and its contents: mannequins, costumes and masks; pastels, pencils and charcoal sticks; tubes of acrylics, traditional oil paint and water-mixable oil.

To the music in your studio: Amalia, Mariza and Camané; Mouloudji, Montand and Patachou; *Rigoletto*, *La Traviata* and *Carmen*.

To 'Kubla Khan' ('For he on honey-dew hath fed, / And drunk the milk of paradise'), always read aloud after dinner – with you joining in – from my old and battered *Albatross Book of Living Verse*, which my father bought me at the Festival of Britain in 1951.

★★

(Paris)
To Géricault's 'Raft of the Medusa' in the Louvre. You would like to do a picture that size. 'The figure there, face down: Delacroix was the model.' 'He was influenced/inspired by Géricault,' you reply. (Which word did you use? Maybe both.)

To the art of Victor Hugo seen in his house, 6 Place des Vosges. You praise the drawings and sketches.

To the paintings and books in the apartment of a poet and a painter, rue Lepic.

To Raymond Mason's sculptures: 'The Crowd' in the Tuileries and 'The Expulsion of Fruit and Vegetables from the Heart of Paris, Feb 28th 1969', in Saint-Eustache Church, Les Halles.

★★

(Lake Orta)
To the life-size terracotta and wooden figures on the Sacro Monte.

(Venice)
To Titian's 'Pietà' in the Accademia: his final painting. You examine it closely.

To the Tiepolo fresco ('here begins modern art', says Raymond Mason, met by chance in the very room) in Ca' Rezzonico, the palazzo where Robert Browning lived and Cole Porter stayed and where visits by Henry James to Browning inspired 'The Private Life'.

To the graves of three Russians, Stravinsky, Diaghilev, Brodsky, on San Michele. You light a candle for your mother in a small chapel.

To the glass-blowers of Murano.

(Florence)
To Donatello's 'Penitent Magdalene' in the Museo dell' Opera dell Duomo.

To Masaccio: Brancacci Chapel in the late afternoon.

To Rilke *oltr'arno*.

To Dostoevsky and the Brownings, whose apartments are close to the Pitti Palace.

★★

(Zurich)
To Valloton's 'Interior with a Woman in Red' and other paintings in the Kunsthaus. "Maybe he influenced Hopper", you say.

To the work of a mask-maker in a village half an hour from the city. You buy one of his masks, now a stalwart prop in the studio.

(Basel)
To Holbein's 'Dead Christ' in the Kunstsammlung. Prince Myshkin in *The Idiot*: 'A man's faith might be ruined by that picture'. Discussing Dostoevsky on the train back to Zurich: for you, his best novel is *The Idiot*, for me, *Brothers Karamazov.*

★★

(Vienna)
To *Don Carlos* at the Opernhaus. Your memories of the box at the Lisbon opera house where you saw *Rigoletto, La Traviata* and *Carmen* and many other operas with your father.

To *The Merry Widow* at the Volkstheater and the coffee houses; their ghosts: Joseph Roth, Freud, Mahler, Arthur Schnitzler, Hofmannsthal, Stefan Zweig, Karl Kraus.

To the 'Venus of Willendorf' at the Natural History Museum and Franz-Xaver Messerschmidt at the Belvedere. To the Albertina, world-famous for its drawings and prints, closed for refurbishment.....

★★

(Madrid)
To Velasquez.

To Goya's 'Black Paintings' and Yves Bonnefoy's book on the artist.

To the paintings of Jose de Ribera in the Academia, an artist you want me to discover.

To Salvador Dali, whom you talk me out of disrespecting, talk me into appreciating.

(Valladolid)
To the museum of painted wooden sculptures which you love.

(Burgos)
To the monastery of alabasters, near the Cathedral with the vast tomb of El Cid.

(Barcelona)
To the early work of Picasso and Miro. To silent thoughts about the early work of other great and life-long painters.

★★

(Antwerp)
To 'the grotesque paintings and drawings' by Goya, Redon and Ensor exhibited in the Museum of Fine Arts.

To the lace you buy in a shop near the cathedral with its enormous Rubens triptych, lace folded neatly in the studio after use.

★★

(Munich)
To 'Lamentation over the Dead Christ', Botticelli's pietà in the Alte Pinakothek. The way you give this troubled and anxious, intense and frightening picture your full attention.

★★

(Colmar)
To Matthias Grünewald's Isenheim Altarpiece.

To Martin Schongauer's 'Madonna of the Rose Garden' in the Church of the Dominicans. We wander to a dark and empty chapel where your eye is caught by an obscure ostensory with two angels. You take out your pencil and sketchbook.

2014/2016

I.   1964–1971

TREE

His ancient moments dropped like leaves:
he trod on one, two...
as a hound picks up the scent,
as a compass comes to rest.

But there were too many leaves
to tread. So he cut down
the tree, and left behind
a memory of broken leaves.

STONES

I disturb them, to be reassured
nothing is beyond me.
They are deeply touched, their night
is untouched by that re-
cognition. I would see
through them, air-tight,
I'm in my element, immured.

THE WAVES

They sweep away pebbles,
seaweed, sand.

The tide recedes. Movement
of pebble is nothing.

There are limits, after all
the beaches.

THE GRAVE

Weather-beaten:

a word
part erased,

Time slowly
lowered
into the ground.

OBSESSION: A STRUCTURE

Uninvited
it pounds inside my head.

Wrong moves collide,
they crack me up, like sticks.

Compressed, a scream
is knotted in my brow.

The stone in my head
kicks like an unborn baby,
bends the mind,
drags me like a ball and chain,
dead weight, slow death.

I shove, in perpetual labour.
Oh to push it out, once and for all:
then I'll have a feast
of deliverance,
throw off my ball and chain
and dance.

I fool
myself that all is possible.

LAND OF ANCIENT MOONS

1.

Your stillness brings back memories of stone
found on forest walks through rain and darkness.
Who shall touch an object for long life?

Ground at last into the earth,
buried alive in that,
you are no longer you
unlike the pebbles you're indifferent to.
I disinter your bones.
You enter into
the spirit of my ruins.

2.

I am the stone you kicked
on the beach of your night:
recognition cracked
my stony silence.

You are the works,
a literal dream,
your voice
soft fruit in ashes;
you danced:
syntax of gesture
translated into image.

3.

Now, absence minded,
you have left
for a land of ancient moons
and yet a sense of you
– ray of nervous energy
slanting to the air –
flickers through the distances
like an event about to be remembered
in the shadow light.

HEATER

Towards the focal point
eyes fix the red,
are drawn into the heat.
Lines emerge into a moment
heater is backdrop to.

Moment after moment,
lines parade,
out of focus until the mind
controls projection.
Too late

to reify the past:
the moments disappear
and eyes withdraw
half expecting credit titles
bold against the heater.

NECESSARY FICTION

The hardened heart of rock was still
beating. That I knew, but did not feel.
I had no choice. Stone change is not
upon a scale the heart of man
can measure. Reason
is party to this ignorance.

But what if what I know is so much air
when feeling does not lie upon
mind's bedrock? And would what is felt
be necessary fiction
as if it were independent of a thought?
I move the rock. It is not moved.

EAST SIXTH STREET, 1966

(from *Poem for L*)

Your pictures speak to me, but not to you
who live alone the tensions they portray.
You laugh at all attempts to read a struggle
into them, and are not drawn. Your room
is full of paintings like your head. Across
the pond I send you books. You send me crayons.
I pause in wonder before the rainbow on
the edge of your heart...

THE SOUND OF THE LAND: REFLECTION

One must have a mind of winter (Stevens)

1.
Through myself, I see
across the road a woman's
head in an upper window.

Such glamour:
that upstairs light
in a distant land

of the mind's eye
shadow-flickers
like a trembling hand.

2.
The hand moves
into the air
behind the window,

spreads itself in
a mysterious
delirium of caresses.

I play the piano,
flow into a remembered
sweetness. My hands
tremble: wrong notes

slice the window,
as if summoned
by that other hand
behind the window.

3.

You are late tonight, maybe you won't come.
I hang suspended, or I walk the waters
of the night, and you, an apparition,
merge with my reflection, on the square:
in little death, let me strike out
along a tangent of oblivion,
serene as stone.
You are late tonight, maybe you won't come.

4.

Storm hits the roof,
anger is in the air.
I hear a baby
scream through the rain.
Has lightning
electrocuted
the black cat in the square
my house gives onto?

CHILDHOOD

The street was whole,
no outside had influence,
no moon to a sea.
It was self-contained like me,
in one-to-one ratio.

I remember imagining
a great bell-jar
might cover
my street against rain
and night. One day,

I felt a sense of *elsewhere*
swirl around my mind like fog,
not to return for many years,
when I recognised the same
meeting with *the other*,

this time within
as I read certain writers,
only a few, how much
they drew me out and back –
the measure of their power.

Ah, my street remained
inviolate until
I was ready at last
to integrate the other:
moon to a sea.

DIMENSION

I live on the edge, on edge.
I balance on a pebble.

I summon a mirage:
connection lost

and lost again.
Shadows curve across

the half-light
of your no-woman's-land,

as in a black and white movie
about a mausoleum of remembrance.

BLACKHEATH: AUTUMN

Absence all around the common,
change is in the air.
A bird is homing somewhere.
The wings of night swoop down,
sweep me
into the shadow of a tree,
whose branch will break.

TO A VOICE

Now all I have is the presence
of the voice behind your face,

voice the colour of your eyes
when drunk you sang to me,

eyes a dream you etched
on the whites of my eyes.

I grasp the shadow of your voice,
like flesh.

I want you
in my no light.

BEACH

Walking blindly
on your beach,

I stumbled
on a pebble.

Your sands
were now rock face.

You were no sea,
palpably.

Shall I kiss life
into the pebble?

FOR ALL WE KNOW

Take your pencils
And draw these faces

Carl Sandburg *(Chicago Poems)*

One softly hinted
she was mortally ill:
a hug, then we walked
down Lake Shore Drive
from Chicago's great museum
before returning
to our separate lives.

One died
within a year
of his leaving
Chicago: drowned
in Italy.
They never found
the body.

One was my lover.
We have not kept in touch.
By now she will have moved
from the South Side
where we ate ice-cream
and did not build
a palace of dreams.

One is now in prison.
He gave me
a set of Billie
Holiday recordings.
Nice work if you can get it.
He was a pall-
bearer at her funeral.

Three years on,
my friends in the town
where I first lived alone
are dead or gone.
Lady Day
is on the record player
as time goes by.

Each waits for the other to come near.
The hurter cannot make the first move
since the silence of the other says
that he has not yet been forgiven.
The hurt one cannot make the first move
since he cannot know the hurter's heart
(nor that his conscience is not troubled
by what he did, only by the hurt)
and what made him do what he has done.

More than anything the hurter wants
what can never be – a *way* to bring
their frames of reference together
that the hurt one may take to his heart.

The hurter thought he had found a way
but now he knows his way *is*, must be
beyond the other's understanding,
if such understanding were ever
possible, with conscience untroubled
through the hurter's acting in good faith.

Eaten by his own light, he burns now,
a secret sharer in the other's hurt.

THE REFLECTION

Not
not-being,
not
being,
not
nothingness

is your
reflection in the mirror
but the
other of being,

is
my reflection
in these words.

RETURN TO ASHKELON

(for CV and i.m. EV)

1.

We pass the orange-groves
surrounded
by cypresses against the wind,

we pass barbed wire not there last year.

2.

In the space of time
we find

a bone
with a flower
growing out of it
a decapitated
terra cotta virgin
lying between
a coffin-nail
and a column of ants
the wedding-
ring of a Philistine
by a heavy
eucalyptus tree

a tiny obol
a bit of glass
the handle of a jug
a broken plate

ruined mosaics
shattered marble columns
and a sheikh's tomb.

3.
Two amorous lizards
embrace in the sand.

4.
I stumble on a coin
shaken to the surface

by rain and wind. We polish it
until reliefs and contours show.

5.
Ah, the season of
the dying of the oranges
is the season of
the budding on the wild vines.

6.
(The Wanderer)

His God still lives and symbols keep
their meaning.
                Drinking from rocks,
splitting the wind, he sings the real,
the poet dances, whose heaven is
quotidian earth where *is* is sacred:
in his language of remembrance
he sings an ancient song of earth.

7.
It was raining. We made a fire on the beach. The flames survived
the rain and the meal we cooked was good. After we had eaten we
smothered the flames with sand. Some charred eggshells and *matsoh*
crumbs remained. They can't have lasted long.

MANIFOLD CIRCLE

Many so-called disturbances are regarded as
pathological in themelves; in fact they can sometimes
be a stage in a healing process.

R.D. Laing

Apparent perfection is
my undoing.

With no line to follow
that does not swallow
itself,

my heads go round in
circles, overlap: the only

way into one
is through another.

I try to stay
around
the first one
is the devil I know:

then what, I try
to leave
it all to itself

but I, that other,
is not the one
and the same old thing.

I am going round my
head is going round
me all around me.

This day,
empty of hours:

vertigo is a white
absence halfway home.

INVISIBLE INK

We have lost our voices.
Silence is

the deepest structure of them all.
If you write me
a letter in
invisible ink

I shall know
how to read between the lines.
We shall look upon each other:
liminal.

PEBBLE

Pebble, 'magic mountain', packed
tight with sediment, with veins
through oceans of a long night.

Pebble: core of rock pool, wind
and rain the sand consumes, chock-
a-block like a diamond, a scream.

Pebble: an energy at one
with being alone, with fear.

Pebble: mirror of your image.

PICTURE ON THE WALL:
NO-MAN'S-LANDSCAPE

(two takes)

1.

A presence tinges my remembering –
not of some event, but that good time's
structure, open-ended, of infinite
dispositions, possibilities, I thought.

It is a house of emptiness, a house
of no gesture, and no flickering
recognition lightens the stillness
within those trees, that fence before the trees,

within the field drawn as another fence:
all is stasis beyond the fated stasis
of the charcoal images of death in life;
the image of unspoken absence speaks.

2.

Cruelty of charcoal:
unpeopled landscape
fraught with hints of terror.
Nothing but a pathway, trees,
fence and winter sky.   '

Disaster scene: before
or after? She's left out
the agents of the deed.
What have they done to her?
What will they do to her?

Truly, a philosopher,
a lover
of the search for wisdom.

His every word is weighed,
he speaks
in such a measured way

you know the words are pulled
back to the centre of his being,
to the crystal.

At the end of meditation,
in the world,
he wills

purity of heart
and peace of mind:
this crystal equilibrium

is not
intended as a guide
for the perplexed

and being single-minded
is his own thing:
inward bound,

still
he holds sway
in the way

of life
of all he comes
in touch with.

EVENING OF THE ROSE

(i.m Paul Celan)

Let the exiles in-gather,
the word has come home:
a memorial prayer
to a place and a name.

As he laid his head
on Shulamith's breast
the unbecoming dead
sang him to his rest.

CHECKPOINT CHARLIE

I put my book on the table,
stretch myself:
I am tired.
The time has come again
for doing what I do
before I am allowed to go to bed.

I switch the record-player off,
pull out the plug
and push the point-switch up.
I tidy my desk
and I tidy it again,
again,
and just before I leave the room
I check the point again.

I switch off the light
and leave the room
and close the door.
And open the door again,
make sure the light's out,
peer beneath the shade
and eye the bulb.

I go back to the door,
switch on the light,
so that I know for sure what's on,
what's off,
then turn out the light again.
And leave the room
and close the door.
And open the door again.

6.30 P.M. ON THE DOT

(For Octavio Paz, London 1971)

Ten seconds later
this *word* in italics
leaves the ink ex-
tension of my hand,

enters the page
a great distance
from the darkness
the word began in.

I borrow from you
stone, move onto
sun, and recall
your poem which "comes

full circle / forever
arriving". I break
through the circle, return
to my own words.

II.　1972–1976

Twelve Fragments

EARLY PHOTOGRAPH OF
MICHAEL HAMBURGER

Found in the distances of childhood
and looking for all the world,
his face floats towards the picture's margin.

PRIMROSE GARDENS, LONDON NW3

We move house tomorrow
and take ourselves with.

SISTER OF THE SEA

(for Avraham Shlonsky)

Once in the valley of Jezreel
you married the sister of the sea
(carpet of seaweed and rocks),
the moon, which is full tonight.

ONION

Cross the lines of a life.
Strip away the layers.
The eye of the storm is closed.

GRANDMOTHER

I hear them knocking
the lid of your coffin
into place. I love you.

MOTHER TONGUE

(for Nathaniel)

He smiles: the interview is over.
Beneath our dialectic is desire
unending, for a language of the mother.

IN MEMORIAM

Veronica Forrest-Thomson 1947–1975

She died before her time: is named the late:
is still a presence, young, *an early night.*

RECOLLECTION

Once by the lake in Chicago I recalled
a walk (long buried) along the Cambridge Backs.
In a space of time I told a time of space.

JOSEPH RUDOLF, 92, SPEAKS TO HIS GRANDSON

'If you interrupt me once more I
shall take away your name'.

MATISSE CHAPEL, VENCE

Synagoga, weep for joy:
this chapel is a holy place.

CARELESS LOVE

You landed on the moon this afternoon.

THE LOST TRIBE

(a poem which came to me in a dream)
for James Hogan, who gave me the title

We are the little people,
patient in our anonymity.

LATE NIGHT

I dismember the lines of your beautiful poem,
like a limb in a terrible experiment.

The cathode swallows Cagney like a whirlpool.
A cat squalls in the back end of the garden.

Silent ghost, the humid night bears down:
The motel bed will vibrate for a quarter.

ENGLAND

1.
Down Grey Street, and Dean Street
past Dog Leap Stairs
to the house
of Bessie Surtees

by the Tyne River.
Here Bessie eloped
with a future
Lord Chancellor.

We enter the frame:
on the first floor
touch the window
she eloped from.

2.
Leave the house through
the back door, then
along and up
winding steps to a point

before the Law Courts,
look back on the house,
all timber and timber,
landscape I cherish.

Wood is for memory,
lined like an ancient,
stained with the presence
of Bessie and unnamed

people I summon.
The frame
decomposes. To the bridge.
To the river.

SONG RECITAL IN A CITY CHURCH

The song of a Jewess returns us
to York's Eden before the expulsion.

This place near-consumed in the Great
Fire of London, once again

consumed by a passion: the voice
of Jerusalem, city of peace...

Drills plough through chartered streets outside:
redeemers of the land live on.

Of old London Bridge, nothing
remains but an arch on dry land.

'TOUT LECTEUR EST L'ÉLU D'UN LIVRE'

1
I loved the man,
I loved the book.

I quarrelled
with the man, as the man
quarrels with his own book always.

Now
I quarrel with the book
twice over.

2

To read again the book
I loved. No.
To read again the book
I loved at a time
when I did this or that:
memory rides rough-
shod over the bones
of our dead
whom we envy.

3 (E. J. speaks to Cavafy, Alexandria 1930)

'You are something of a Jew, Cavafy,
like all poets. Before the crystal night
fragments to stars, will you not walk across
the crooked street to Morpheus your lover,

who awaits you in his attic, with no pain?
Will your mind not want, upon the midnight,
to flicker with the image of the Lighthouse,
memorial candle shining till the dawn?

Cavafy, write a poem on Caligula,
a kaddish for the Jews he killed in pogroms
here. This is no city for young men.
I live between your lines. Old man, I love you'.

REVEILLE

Rise and shine
with the light:

half-light inside,
outside half-light
enter each other.

All is window.
All is shadow.

DUBROVNIK POEM

1. (Emilio Tolentino speaks)

'Always the Jew was treated
well, in this part of the world.
From Venice we came, from Spain.
Žudioska Ulica,
this street, the Jews have lived in
always. You see the grilles?
Behind them the women sat,
entering the dark space
by way of our house next door.
My family has cared for
the synagogue from there
for over three hundred years.'

'Six hundred years it has stood,
this synagogue on this street.
Now ten women are left,
seven men: not even a *minyan*.
When we returned from Auschwitz
the archives had disappeared:
plundered, stolen, destroyed.
Hidden under floorboards,
some we retrieved, some treasures.'

2. (Restaurant in the old city)

At dinner I talk Russian with a man
from Sarajevo: he tells me
only bears and Christians want to live in
his town in winter when it rains like England.

3. (old city)

Here even reconstructed sites
are beautiful. I see the lights

flash across the new old wall
behind the narrow streets, recall

cities I love. I do not name
them in their holiness of time.

A PRESENCE

Le désir du vrai lieu est le serment de la poésie

Yves Bonnefoy

Leaving my study
where I have spent hours
re-living the quest
of one I translate,

I walk in half-light
across the green hall
between Venetian mirror
and Bavarian clock

to our bedroom: I see
you lying in shadow,
under the masked
clown on the wall,

reading a book,
and of my presence
you know nothing.
I return to the time

of another, his
place and his night
and of my presence
I know nothing.

EMPTY HOUSES

The house is full of absence.
The spider's web of memory
hangs down from all the ceilings.
In the windows' urn
the nightingales of silence
are imprisoned.
Sleeping preludes await
the hour of return.

Shadow's dust
clings to the cloths
on the walls.

In the stopped clock
the minutes have committed suicide.

Ernesto Lopez-Parra (1895–1941)

THE TRANSLATOR ADDRESSES BORGES

(variation on the theme of 'Empty Houses')

Your presence overflows
with memories
of lost memories.

Your prelude
embraces your coda.
Your shadow

clings to your shadow.
Your mind
is the footprint of your mind.

In the clock of you
the minute hand
holds the hour hand,

for all
time: you have
my word for it.

D R E A M   T I M E

Through the train
window I see

another train
meandering through
cities and plains,

to a vanishing point
of no return

beyond the furthest
reaches of night,
of all longing.

I walk across the park,
across the day, humid, foreign,
to the orangery.

The merest
hint of breeze, of rain
announces
perfection or a mood I thought
dead for ever, like a dead
woman, or something uttered in vain.
Inside the orangery:
no hint of breeze, of rain,
announces
perfection or a mood I used to think
dead for ever, like a dead
woman, or something
uttered in the merest
hint of breeze, of rain

as I walk back
across the park,
across the day, humid, foreign.

Once more I name a city
                  where the stone
inspired a life, a life inspired the stone.
It was a place whose 'moral shape.... and moulds
of commonwealth' revealed themselves within
its walls of refuge, where a life was lived,
not happiness pursued, though peaceable
you died, assured of continuity.

Now it is thanks to commerce that the old
place survives, and thanks to commerce will
die tomorrow. Why complain of that,
since this reprieve is after-life? The ancient
city yields the time before a poem.

Our house is always open to the sun
beating on a wall.
                It is a time
of signs....

Before the entrance is the pleasure-
garden of the loveliest
museum: I look, I am entranced.
The text restores attention to
a metamorphosis, the way
all reflection doubles back
upon itself, a mirror-image
and my strategic pose seen through.
I listen hard – the metalanguage
of stone is under-

                stood by grass:
such elemental purity!
such inter-diction, fatal lack
of flaw in evidence. I pass
by the Calder mobile danced
by the wind. Before the pond
and the geometries beyond
sits a dog as immobile
and silent as a Balthus cat.
I go in. To the Balthus. Smile.
The little tiger smells a rat.

CHAGALL

(Museum in Nice)

Horizon
of remembrance,
vault of
childhood: his images
strike home,
old stories well up.

Jacob and the angel
clarified
in the burning
bush of memory.

We leave,
like Adam and Eve,
this artificial
paradise: it
is in the nature
of things,
like a rock water
is struck
from.

BALTHUS

1

His virgins meditate, they stare into
the space of time, dream in the light of day.

Said (wrongly) to be 'the painter', his cats
sit around the colour, at a stroke.

I look upon the dream of his Thérèse
(the cats sup milk), whose thighs are open to

'the world': at last I understand that if
we are not – and we are not – *voyeurs*

then we are Thérèse. I catch the eye
of the girl beside me. I am Thérèse,

innocent, pure and exiled adolescent
dreaming exile, purity and innocence.

2

He draws the light, the sting of memory.
Repose accuses, stillness calls. The silence

of a Balthus virgin screams across
the centuries to Piero and Mantegna.

She whispers, whispers to herself that no
action shall be sister to the dream.

Three Poems of the Grave

POWER CUT

(i.m. Rabbi Michael Goulston 1931–1972)

I write
in darkness
to music
on the air.
My friend,
dying in
hospital,
drinks milk
endlessly.
His death
means the world:
friends throw
handfuls
of earth in-
to the grave.

IN HIS DEATH

In his death
they let him down

slowly, carefully
into the grave

and shovel earth
over him

to share the blame
as it is said

in his life
they let him down

KAFKA'S TOMB

*Yesterday I found the grave. If you look for it timidly it's really
almost impossible to find.*

I ask my friend to visit Kafka's grave.
She finds the cemetery.
She climbs the fence.
Impossible
to identify the tomb.

Stumbling through the undergrowth she asks
two boys which is the grave.
They smile.
They flap their arms.

PRAYER FOR KAFKA AND OURSELVES

(3: vi: 1924)

We walk alone on our roots
in Prague, dead centre of Europe.

Golem's dream, tears of stone.

We are the children of Kafka.

The stone the builders rejected
has become the corner stone.

AMSTERDAM

Here, late at night, the ground floor window
is open to the world, and now I under-
stand Vermeer.
                    Even as the girl
moves about the room she is still life.
Her cat is motionless.
                    I name it Balthus.

Beyond, train after train moves out
of this city for another city.
Beside, the canal is filled with works:
a necessary evil gone along with
before I cross the bridge just as I reach it.
Beside, a house empty of all
it had ever filled;
                    framework without
and oh, the loneliness of surface structures.

Ahead, my hotel room where memories
are framed; aided, abetted by the text.

Here by the ground floor window is
a mirror, where the girl may see the world
and not be seen seeing: we under-
stand each other. Here
                    Dutch life
reveals art: is text; Vermeer draws Balthus.

A HISTORY OF SILENCE

I said things
that never were,

to reach a new
language was my object.

*

I write things
that were

to reach an ancient
language I know not.

★

I shall speak the white night of
the blood of martyrs

and write
a history of silence.

EDWARD HOPPER

Objectivists are metaphysical.
Over against the stillness of the house
what is not still need not be on the move.
And yet, upon my word, the absence moves
to the presence, by the railroad, of the house.
Reality? No way into this house
that is nothing but a structure of his mind
painted alone because it was not there.

Z. KOTOWICZ READING BACHELARD ON A TRAIN

Half-awake
in the empty carriage
he almost sets
his jacket alight
with a cigarette;
half-asleep, he sees,
in the window, someone
swift, nervous,
striking him:
ah, it is he himself
on the other side,
gesturing
in the twilight;
the tiny flame
pinpoints a space
for reverie

THE SAME RIVER TWICE

(J.C.B. Angel Court, 1964)

He took my words.
                    Without a word
he changed the order of my things.
Still my poem, just about.
Much water has flowed by.
                    No word.
But to this day, ten years on
I write the same words.
                    The end
of all my words is a beginning.

REDEMPTION SONG

(after abandoning a translation)
For Richard B

Between sign
and sign:

second
coming of language,

presence under-
written by text,

signature of origin,
re-signed,

spoken in tongues,
what's bruited,

noise abroad
the wording's wrong:

word of mouth
makes nothing happen,

Chinese whisper,
blind eye

mindful of absence,
unwriting

implodes in
the name of action

LAST POEM OF KARL KRAUS (1936)

Don't ask what I've been doing all the time.
I hold my tongue;
and I shan't say why.
And there is a stillness when the earth cracks.
No word fitted;
I speak only in my sleep,
and dream of a laughing sun.
This too will pass;
afterwards it makes no difference.
The word passed away when that world woke up.

EMMA VAN NAME

Emma, what is in a name?
Your creator of no name
gave us the immortal name

my eyes reflect. They see
that you are good. Oh Emma,
fecund infanta, baboushka,

had your local habitation
been my own, I would have named you
little mother of the earth.

III.   1977–1991

ANCIENT OF DAYS

To die old
like a late night:

the aged man,
ancient of days,

is tired and tired
and none

shall make him afraid.
He walks

humbly before
God and returns

to his village
where nothing

remains but one oak
broader

than six
men in a ring.

AGAINST ANXIETY

i.m. Walter Benjamin

Write the history
of a poem

in a poem.
Take one poem:

some time before,
another poem

tracks forth;
another poem

some time after
tracks back:

what are the three
poems if not

emanations,
ruins

of the all-poem,
the harmony

Messiah
(whose name

God created
before he created

the world)
will reveal?

'THE TRUE INFLECTIONS...'

(Hayward Gallery, London June 1978)

1

I stand before an Auerbach picture.
She stands before an Auerbach picture.

She moves on to the space
in a partition where the door should be.

Behind her, through the window, realistic
buses cross the bridge.

2

She walks towards a picture;
she views it from some angles:

Participant observer, unaware,
in a voyeur's network of perception,

she is Auerbach's mirror,
reflected in his mind's eye.

PICTURE AT AN EXHIBITION

('Old London Bridge' by Sir Samuel Scott,
exhibited at Somerset House 1977)

The river is the mother of the city.
Over and over the bridge takes Londoners
to London from London, plays both ends
against the middle.
                                    'Halfway' through my life
in a house on that good bridge I am
a small boy, stand alone, and watch a small
boat move underneath my house, as late
cries from one bank mingle with new lights
from the other.
                        It is impossible
not to want to linger on this music.
Remembrance is coloured in the making.

INVOCATIONS FOR A WORK IN CLAY

Mother of lightning,
queen of the salamanders,

sexual mound
of the Buddha woman,

mouth, an eye,
amulet of the spheres,

disaster,
your lodestar's no,

for a good season,
for a break in the day.

AUTUMNAL

Sun sets the scene of quiet *without*: the land.

Within: the mind: they merge.

Only ruin imagines perfection.

Only life imagines music.

The word *sun* sets the scene, the name of cry.

ANCIENT BEAMS

Thatch Cottage, Great Waldingfield

What is it about you
asks I read in you an image
of support as if I'm the wall
you, in your presence, edge through?

Quite, quite. Just so. Yes indeed.
I am what is about you.
Would I were you to see
through myself, see myself through.

Let me (truly, like one of
the beams) pray at my angle
to the universe, that the truth
shall ever be told aslant.

It has taken my fancy
to bring us together. Therefore
the poem insists I enter
into the spirit of things.

HALFWAY THROUGH LIFE

(after Hölderlin)

Yellow with pears, and full
of wild roses, the land
sinks into the lake,
O gracious swans,
and drunken with kisses
you dip your heads
into the sober, hallowed water.

Ah, where shall I find, when
winter comes, the flowers, and where
the sunshine and
the shadows of the earth?
Speechless and cold
stand the walls. In the wind
the weather-vanes clatter.

PARMERDE JUNPHE 1872

et libre soit cette infortune (Rimbaud)

How shall I know for certain there is no past
to meet with, no future for the dead
poet, save in his writing? I shall know

when I discover the bedroom with a view
(rue Monsieur-le Prince) he wrote about
in a letter to his school-friend Delahaye.

I shall look out of the narrow window
giving onto a garden of the Lycée Saint-Louis
and alone at last with the "infernal bridegroom"
cry out: reveal yourself, return, attend

the word of one already older than you
when you'd written your season in hell, and breakfast
with me on wine, sun, bread, tobacco...
There, mocked by your silence, yes I shall know.

CATALOGUE SONNET

I am determined by my class
I am determined by my sex
I am determined by my God
I am determined by my genes
I am determined by my unconscious
I am determined by my childhood
I am determined by my death
I am determined by my climate
I am determined by my homeland
I am determined by my work
I am determined by my newspaper
I am determined by my deep linguistic structures
I am determined by my etcetera
I am determined to be free

OLD MAN

(Joseph Rudolf: born 1880 or 1882, died September 2 1980)

Old man,
         you governed
my life.
        I wanted
to write you,
           your life.
What for?
          Who for?
My daughter's daughter?
Your seed unto?

Oh, you did well
to leave,
        what
did you know
of the clock
approaching midnight?

Less light.
         Less
light.
      No more
poems; and what
returns
for our pains;
          sleep
Joseph, sleep,
          face up,
lad's love.

PROCESS VERBAL

for Lorine Niedecker

To sense
and sound
this world:

event I'd
not been stirred
by:
the word
eventide

READING STEVENS IN HOSPITAL

The malady of the quotidian

I read each phrase, each line, re-read
the one before, the next, one more
each time, the way I always do –
the only way to read this 'man

whose pharynx was bad', this seamster:
I am – unravelling the coat
of many colours – his undoing.
A seeming sense it, all, is.

Reading, writing, I am inter-
rupted by well-meaning fellow
patients offering this or that.
It takes all sorts to unmake worlds.

VASKO POPA IN CAMBRIDGE

'Emperor priest':
I learn with a master.

Speaking in French,
we exchange proverbs.

He tells me a story
about a lame wolf.

I go native,
howl with the wolves.

IN MEMORIAM

(Nadezhda Yakovlevna Mandelshtam)

In a dark time
your husband
Lazarus arose
because you remembered
all his words.
This is your end
but he lives on.
You made an ark.
'All poets are Jews'.
Hope and the poem
are one, as you
stand in a queue.
Now a *noem*
tells and retells
how one man became
an expert in farewells.

ET IN ARCADIA EGO

for MMG

Imagine dead
imagine you
dying in other
words, living
in your room your
friend says is
not of this world,
where you write
world's end,
at the epi-
centre of London,
together, centred,
much married
to your words,
your friends your
opposite numbers
dying to
dying of
dying for
the same thoughts:
overkill?
ground zero?
collateral damage?:
the rest is
eternal,
silence of four
minutes.

NOONDAY

to S

Edging the meridian
he arrived before his time.
'You're early, love'. She laughed.
'I'm sorry'. And her eyes.

'Hurry slowly'. And he did.
Describe the circle in one line.
A heart is on the line,
takes the two words to itself:

he did not kiss her, she
kissed him. 'The spoils of noon'.
Slow on his lips. Was that what
it was? One thing he knew he...

His bones live... 'Write a poem
in my garden, and do not
fall in love unless I say so'.
Upon the mid-day: second

half of life, if life be given,
light years take away four minutes
in the year without a summer,
on the threshold where she moves

and does not move. Still and all
his word poised for ever on
the point of what. O never known,
this unicorn, this 'pilgrim soul'.

HEADLAND

My son, my daughter,
alone by the sea
run, run to the end
of what they are.

Nearby, I shiver
in the wet sand,
the sun also
at its nadir.

The cold wind blows
hard on my head.
I run, run to
the beginning

of what I am.
I raise up my eyes.
The lowly sun
has disappeared.

This place is called
the headland.

BREUGHEL TO AUDEN

For A.W.

Our daily work is touched by
as it touches
the seasons of the year,
is touched on by the seasons,
touched with.

You poets you
plough on
regardless.

POEM-EM

(Michael Michaeledes)

Your reliefs
frustrate.
Unto them I do not do
as I would be done by:
I want them
not upon the wall. I want them
free-floating like mobiles.
I want to walk
around them.

In a space like the space
they create inside my head
where I walk
around my thoughts
cleansed of ancient signs
and dead would nots
and dead wood knots

(Coloured
square within
coloured square within coloured
square broken into
triangles
the line a lightning
flash)

How dare I want them
other than they are.
Pure and simple
these things do their thing.
In their no-man's-land
they work
their passage as they are.
This is a relief
not a frustration.

IV   1992–2013

ANTIQUE LAND

Again
the sea, always an end

seven nights away
seven days away

the sun goes down
a boat
passes the balcony
to the sound of
waves breaking on
rocks

the sea, always a beginning
again

YOU, PAINTING

You, painting,
are a literal
photograph, drawn
in light,

water from
the well of presence.

I, poem, envy
you your open
secret: mind's eye's
working of light
the word light
stands for;

words: those
things you
do not stand for.

Death is a circle reduced
to a point. Eaten alive
Fran can't bear the weight. Only
a little longer. Wait. Now

lighter than air she hovers
a song bird in her silence,
dark, still, a sated lover.
Her son Seth places a rose

husband Clive places a rose
on the wooden box. Goodbye,
he gently pats the box.
Gathered by the *Shekhina*

Fran is one with flame and rose.
The point is…. a circle, grows
and her birdsong is written,
like a new moon, in the sky.

BONNARD: THE LAST PICTURE

From the window
in my bedroom,
the almond tree,
in blossom,

looks like a juggler
a peacock
a dancer
..... I cannot work on,

too weak.
It needs, the picture
needs, retouching,
bottom left, green's wrong.

Who told me,
was it Jarry,
the Kabbala says
'the road

to paradise
is by way
of the almond tree'?
A nice

thought in my position.
Does the dog
need retouching too?
If you lean

against
the almond's trunk
and shake
the blossom

off the branches,
a poet is
translated.
Now

cover
the mirror,
draw conclusions.
Close my eyes.

IN MEMORIAM GISÈLE CELAN-LESTRANGE

Zhivago,
zealot's élan,
estranged.

She his
unwriter is
that she is,

prints
a light unto
the benighted,

her eye
for a thou,
ci-gît

(Va.
Go.) No
man's land.

COLOMBINE AT THE PICASSO EXHIBITION, PARIS, NOVEMBER 1996

She leaves me at the photographs
to reapply
herself to the paintings.

Soon enough, I follow her
to the portrayal
of Salvado dressed as Harlequin:

'See the way Picasso
uses distemper:
I can learn from him'.

I observe
how well she looks
at what

is seen
to be the case in point:
a mirror image.

BRANCA'S VINEYARD

(At Terceira in the Azores)

The sleeping passion of volcanic stone
on the shore of Biscoïtos senses
in its deep dream the agony of whales
hunted through these waters. In Branca's Vineyard
the grapes are drowsy, sheltered in the heat
emanating from volcano soil.
I drink the wine a painter of the sacred
and doctor of the heart pressed into being,
then, for a moment, lingering alone,
wineglass in hand, pen upon this paper,
inhale an ancient oneness which I'd thought
lost for all time, except when I make love
with the woman who has just spoken to me
and broken the spell, as spells are always broken.

Biscoïtos, 17 May 1998

(thirteen ways of looking at Pierre Rouve)

1
A voice across the air
waves: is anybody there?

2
Big brother
is watching his sister.
'I am a draft of her.
I said *brouillon*
not *bouillon*'.

3
Amid the perfected
follies of schoolmen
he riffs and raps.

4
Drinking plum brandy,
smoking a fag,
he wonders
what the past will bring.

5
To amuse
his young daughter
he juggles his hats.
To amuse
his wife (a muse)
he wears them all at once.

6)
Every day
he lives on 'the bread
of faithful speech'.
Metaphysical dread
has no right of way.
His wife skins a peach.

7)
Even a fox
knows one big thing
at the end of the hunt.

8)
After a time
I contact
Pierre: we meet
in his studio:
eye contact
under the gaze
of his icon.
We see
eye to eye.

9)
Soccer is a passion,
he keeps his eye on
the ball:
he's never been known to miss
a professional foul.

10)
Strapped to the mast,
unlike Turner
he studies the structures
of the back-burner.

11)
Arresting time
with a moving image
he writes his love in light.

12)
This *bougre* has been summoned
to the heavenly academy.
He orders a *demi*
and engages in battle
with Stevens and Mallarmé.

13)
The exile now
looks homeward,
father reborn
under the hidden moon.

REMOVAL MAN

(Natalie Dower's paintings)

I make a move
to go
back to the one
that moves me
most,

a deep
content, something
between us,
call it trust,
call it touch –
removes me
to another plane.

I take the point. I want
to tell it
like it is,
without
measure,
all proportions
guarded,
the secret
number of your art,
the code
beneath the screen.
You draw me in,
thoughts
coloured
by desire. I
am a fly
on the wall of your

mind, set
against
disorder.
I am
before you, your work,
you work on,
your subject.

This was my move.
I empty my
head to a vacuum
that I may leave
room.

CIRCLE OF KNOWLEDGE

Flying west has dislocated me
and space has been converted into time.

On my watch it's seven in the morning.
On my body it's noon in Kentish Town
where you are at work, humming white noise
to distract distraction,
the presence of a model notwithstanding.

Here in Miami, not in town, spaced out,
I miss you by miles, by hours, *mon amie*.

ARCHITEXTURE

(Julia Farrer at the Eagle Gallery, London)

Walking around the room
I try to take
my bearings, the measure
of your work,
try to find
your story: line and colour
play each other,
each plays
into the other,
measure for measure,
and yet, what could be
more serious
than this comedy?

You, lady,
I know are
playing for high stakes:
I measure my words:
the only line you follow
is your own,
yet the human clay
does not end
with your hand,
for your brush,
playing mind games,
kisses what
was deadly still
into movement,
after the "happy"
mistakes you come by
accidentally

on purpose.
Your pictures
mirror the image
of their making:
they sing
the thin line
between two people
that divides
old misunderstandings
from the deep
where both are on the level
for good and all.

Configured, your work
suggests
metamorphosis
of a gestalt,
your figuration
a music.
"Architexture"
I borrowed
from Nathaniel Tarn,
restore it
herewith, gathering interest
as a wordless art
holds the line,
melody and descant
in a single voice.

Upstairs lived
my rocking horse

until I was
too big to ride him.

Then my sister
Ruth took over,

then my sister
Mary rode him,

then my sister
Annie rode him.

All the children
rode him, rode him,

swaying forwards,
swaying backwards

until he went
into a cupboard.

One day my mother
threw him out:

off you go: the knackers yard
is the only place for you!

Hold your horses,
mother dear,

Rocky's mine,
he lives forever

In *souvenance*.
Those ancient days........

'DAMASIO ABSTRACTED'

*(Catalogue Sonnet for Dr Tulp and Rembrandt,
announcing the birth of B. Spinoza, 1632)*

My mind is made up of images.
My mind is made up of sensations.
My mind is made up of desires.
My mind is made up of emotions.
My mind is made up of feelings.
My mind is made up of perceptions.
My mind is made up of representations.
My mind is made up of ideas.
My mind is made up of thoughts.
My mind is made up of relationships.
My mind is made up of essences.
My mind is made up of existences.
My mind is made up.
Please do not confuse me with the facts.

FINAL PROOF

And the dust returns to the earth as it was
                    – from the Jewish burial service

(for Jon Glover and i.m. Jon Silkin)

In the East End
stonemason's showroom
I read, re-read
(final proof,

the poet is dead)
the large letters
outlined on
'John' Silkin's tomb-

stone, the writer's
own words included:
'the word surrounded
so by light'.

As it is said,
zihrono l'vraha:
may his memory
be for a blessing.

(Buried along with Jon,
some old prayer
books). Of one thing
I am dead

certain – see, his word
is written stone –
'*Yochanan ben-Yosef,*
Poet', remains

of a poet,
something, indeed.
I bury myself
in his late poems.

UNTER DEN LINDEN

Well, they are gone, and here must I remain,
this lime-tree bower my prison, and the name
of the avenue a trigger for my thoughts
about the places where our paths would cross:

Indica, Turret, Voice Box, Lamb and Flag,
and now friends' funerals. Only last week,
we shook hands at the crematorium
in Hoop Lane (home to the ashes of the man

whose hyper-real sculpted image freaked
first-time visitors to Turret Bookshop),
and said goodbye with Horovitz and Brownjohn
to 'Barnet Finkelstoen', Bernard Stone.

You recalled I'd brought you Rabbi Hugo Gryn's
book to read in hospital, and I tell you
Hugo's buried across the road, escort you
to the Jewish cemetery, a "stoen's" throw

from Bernard's coffin, to inspect the grave
of this man you admired fiercely. And now
for thee, my gentle-hearted Eddie, *to whom
no sound is dissonant which tells of life,*

talk of my gift – before our friend was ashes –
was a reminder you'd survived the knife,
that we are guests at a life-long party thrown,
some say, by the Almighty, Lord of Hosts.

So, drink to life until our bullet's numbered
and may the Lord have mercy on our ghosts.
But not yet, Eddie Linden, always first
with the news, bursting in on Nuttall's reading

to announce that Ezra Pound has died:
'We've all moved up one, then', he replied.
In the firing line, who's next? *And now
my friends emerge / beneath the wide wide heaven.*

FOUND POEM

*Never celebrate the truth in the place where you find it
because it is no longer there*

– Hassidic saying

At the time I knew I'd lost it:
I did not buy the book about
Morandi which I hoped would trigger
the poem that would go with others
written on the subject of
my reaction to a painter, loved.

I'd been mean. It cost me dear
and served me right: example of
not yielding to impulse. That
poem was lost for ever... now
this one – which I found by chance
in MoMA's shop while looking for
a book on Kitaj shortly after
realizing Reinhardt's black
touches on the blue of Klein –
gives me pause for thought: it's poems
written that are lost for ever,
unwritten ones always remain
to be found. Like Morandi
painting variations on
the same theme, it has taken me
twenty years to get the picture.

Two Linked Poems for Charlie

1) DUNEDIN: BOTANICAL GARDENS

Early afternoon, back end of summer:
reading, as it happens, Baxter's poem
'Travelling to Dunedin' and listening

to the City Jazz Band playing 'Moaning',
I feel an urge to annotate this moment
even before my little grandson Charlie

runs over from the children's playground
to present me with a yellow leaf.
I thank him and I place it in

my Baxter book, where it will survive
pressed tight like my heart when I go home
and miss Charlie something rotten.

I stand up and twirl him (heavier than
my full suitcase) round, and know at once
I've done my back in for love of Charlie.

I feel an urge to cross the water,
partly because I'm reading Katherine Mansfield,
partly because it's my way to release

a sense of 'holy nothingness',
here in the space between my Charlie fortnight
and the London flight from Sydney later.

On the ferry to Day's Bay,
sun hot, wind high, ride bumpy: I think about
this morning's drive to Dunedin Airport:

sitting next to Charlie, I suggest
we make a list (as in a children's story)
of the places that we visited together:

'Chinese Garden', Charlie offers first;
I ask him where we heard the music playing:
'Botanical Gardens. I gave you a leaf'.

Mind is dancing
like a drunken woman.

Mind is a thing of strange beauty
like a nightmare sunset.

Mind yearns for freedom
like a hound at the end of its tether.

Mind is imbricated
like a page of Talmud.

Mind betrays itself
like a slip of the tongue.

Mind is all over the place
like a failed intuition.

Mind is broken
like a promise of worse things to come.

Mind overflows
like a darkness of the heart.

Mind takes the plunge
like Empedocles.

Mind overtakes itself
like a surrealist's bicycle.

Mind is neither here nor there
like no-man's-land.

Mind is pregnant with meaning
like a draft poem...

I leave your flat, you know
I'll look up to see you waving
from the first-floor window,
as I walk backwards
to my car, swaying,
flapping my hands, hiding
behind the pillar box.
A couple with a baby
ask if I'm in love.

In my car, I open
the window, wave to your wave,
turn left as slowly
as I can. Your arm slowly
disappears from sight.

My heart sinks. I miss you
already, as I drive
north, passing the house
where my mother died:
ancient memories
return, aslant, to roost.

Back home, I drink red wine
and play Amalia: you phone
and hear her voice. We call
time on the day, and go
to our beds: Eça – who else? –
for you; for me a page of Proust.

V   Two Long Poems

MANDORLA

1

Freeing the line it makes
its entry
edging the eye
away:
a piece only
of my mind
yields
peace of mind
only the time it takes
to settle down
up
the image.

2

Straight up across
round [here] about

both sides a-
gainst the middle

centred parting
silvered lining

geometry
rules OK. Out

the frame up yours
not to reason

the intellect
out of the seen.

3
I dolmen
here I go

again. Stele
configured

totem pole
axed feeling

over grid,
grand is not

the name of
the roll, say

rather a
reversal

levellers
play the field.

4
The principles are out in force today.

O mega-wonderful Romeo-Alfa

a two-way mirror turns into itself.

Once and for all the problematic of
mind/body is resolved. O have a heart

well wicked man, a trial by ordeal
soul owner in your double-breasted suit.

Trading in future perfects I'll come through
liminal transit. Darling wave to me.

5
Heart's eye, give
us a break,

nay-sayers
on a roll.

Freud's essay
'when I say

No, I mean...'

Loch in kop,
who needs it?

Learn the lines
By heart's eye.

6
Ring the changes
on the straight and narrow:
use of bow and arrow
on rifle ranges.

String me along
a heavenly kite,
malingerer
in *ewigkeit*.

7
Plane sailing
over a sense
of site, wave
goodbye, farewell
to the verbals,
talk, who's looking?

8
An I for a Thou
one to one
and the other
way round
a kind of two
you thou
thou you
compassion and intelligence
at one.

9
Same difference
on the margin
grey area,
between the dog
and the wolf
in the country
of old moons.

Wind, oh
still night
window
starlight.

10
A reaching out
across into
and back
again. Rows
of dots read
both ways, an open
field, unlined.
Lines push
forward. Illus.
by trait. The dots

before my eyes,
I read between
the lines. Farra-a-
go-go, galore.

11
How they are and are
not the image, more
into and out of
each other's field
a series, discrete
begin here, and roll on
like eternity,
immaterial
anti-matter, natch:
game, set, lighted match.

12
Minimal
to the point
of
what is
spaced out,
doubt
high
on the line,
therefore it is.

13
Two-step
two time
the faithful,
poetical feat
of clay
to the ear.

14
Contain the vista
belle vue
second site
dialectical : insight
or outsight,
behind
the mirror, turn
the tables,
all bets off.

15
Give them a twist
a flick of the wrist
angelus novus
coming
for to
carry us
(over the
threshold)
home.

16
Cross doubt
crossed out

all over
the place.

All over.

1996/2007

ZIGZAG
(Teaching Autobiography, 2000–2003)

It is the life (M.C.)

1   *Taste and See*

Where we find ourselves
is a magnetic field
not a classroom. Please note,
our ambition is

to trigger the writing
of our own texts.
Before we get going,
some words are in order

concerning the past:
the novel begins
in the seventeenth century
but our subject needs more

time to get going:
focus on feelings
and their individuals
vis-à-vis nature,

society and God,
introspection about
identity, the self.
Old structures no longer

tell you who you are,
fragments of you
survive in the memory
of your children, with *luck*

in what you wrote.
Are you 'merely'
excavating or
constructing under

the influence of
the fiction of your day?
Does the work
of "self-writing"

(timetable jargon)
require danger?
If we do not
experience shame,

are we cheating? Our actions,
or actions reflected
upon: they 'self-stand',
hidden in language,

crying out for attention,
oh, taste and see
they were bad.
Is every work

always a work in
progress or should we
beware revision? We trust
those who admit

fallibility, who
own up to lying.
If the past (and indeed
the future) is 'cities

from a train', the cities
are still there;
the train too, maybe.
Do you remember

a chat in a train,
a book you read? Where
is the memory?
Nowhere until

you've written it down.
Writing it down
at last you find out
who you were,

make sense of
who you are,
rather than explain
some anterior essence.

2   *Zigzag*

The best writers are
the best readers. Writing
is the most intense
reading of the world.

It teaches us to tell
truthfulness from truth.
Our life is lived in zigzag
or concentrically.

It is not lived as story
but told to ourselves
as story, therefore
the text of the story

can be linear
when written, although
you must be aware
of the logical fallacy

known as 'post hoc
ergo propter hoc'.
You're the main character,
a fictional construct

and your text has to live
as writing, that is,
in language. Only then
can it be trusted,

despite its display
of feeling, its mask
of candour. As you go
along, you are making

sense of your self,
not describing a known
quantity like
an I (or a thou).

In this very making,
In this very sense,
the self is the world-
history of your soul:

it is what is told.
This is telling.
Make sure an erratum
slip is inserted

but even the careless
can tell us a truth
about what it is
to be human. Therefore

why not write fiction
instead of the other?
Later, we shall
return to this question

for truth is non-causal
or multi-causal;
truth is provisional:
performative, cognitive.

3   *Double Helix*

Convey the texture
of life or a sense
of meaning or both:
double helix: an inter-

twining, a mutual
modification
inside the chain
of feelings, events.

Own up to 'negative'
factual details,
not in order to
put yourself down,

but in the service
of truth about feelings
via senses and meanings.
Classical object

-ivity is not
at odds with the personal.
After all, we live forwards
and understand backwards.

Integrity of language
houses the truth.
Why be surprised
that the best autobio-

graphies are written
by *writers*, because
ideas and things
only enter into

the spirit of books
by means of the word.
Use words to embody
The history of

your insider dealings:
invoke the workings
of your spirit, the workings
of your mind, bring out

subconscious and non-
rational matters,
posit the structures
of feeling against

outer experience
in language we share,
believe in, remember.
Convey the objective

perceptions of self-
discovery when young,
convey evolution
of spirit. Remember

crafty art counters
sentimentality,
tempers whatever
is *merely* subjective.

4   *Innocent of all Charges*

Use prose as a matrix
for poems, or use
poems as a matrix
for prose. Who am I

to write the self
if the self is
a coalition of
mini-selves or

sub-personalities?
Sure, the identity
of the self is
narrational and

the sun also rises,
our daily bread.
This too is a story.
You don't have to be

wake-minded to know
we do not possess
an ultimate self,
a self that is master

and yet, all the same,
of the self one can say
it's the whole thing *there*,
for objectivists are not

(as I once wrote in error)
metaphysical.
Let us not mock
the post-modernist for

discovering that she
or he runs on the fuel
of selfhood if
at stake is a pension

or court-room verdict.
We are, are we not,
our stories, are spoken
by a character

actor. The self is
a palimpsest. Writing
leads to thought and
memories; memories

and thought do not lead
to writing, not in
that way of course!
Once in a while

we ask ourselves what
the writer left out.
For the most part
we don't mind. What we

have to go on
goes on in language
for fiction can only
privilege what's virtual.

It's not (yet) a crime
to think about a crime.
Facts are events
under description.

The imagination is
innocent of
all charges. We are
haunted by the lives

our parents did not
lead. And what of
the stories of all,
for whatever reason,

lacking a voice?
These beg to be told –
we trust that the tellers
do their inventing

only in language –
while autobiography
speaks the story
of the voice that is heard

telling a story
reborn, re-remembered
in life on the page,
enchanted by virtual

accuracy.
Yes, 'it is the life'
as we don't say
in English.

5   *Not in front of the Children*

This we discovered
late in the day:
"Straight" facts are not
the name of the game

in fiction. Fit out
your wholly invented
characters with
true details taken

from real people:
mix and match, trick or treat,
and, some would say,
on with the motley,

invent the whole lot.
But nothing will work
unless you confront
fear and shame: which is not

to say fiction is
an exercise in
morbidity or
Narcissus on screen.

This does not imply
that writing is psycho-
therapy in
the guise of another

discourse, cross-dressed.
In fiction, kill off
other selves, other others.
The real: próject

as desire, desire
projéct as the real.
Is it true that forbidden
feelings are better

dealt with in music?
If that is the case
do not write about
('in front of') the children

if you have any sense:
no poem or story
is worth it. *Nicht wahr?*
Certain dark thoughts

shall remain in the darkness,
afloat in a sea
of self-love, in a night
mirror, a foetus

safe in its mother's
belly. Remember
once the story is told,
it loses potential,

the virtual is gone
for good, as it were.
If poetry is
vertical then

fiction must be
horizontal. Between
memory and language
falls the structure.

6   *The Face beneath the Mask*

In light of now,
the past, like the future,
can't be predicted,
for the child becomes

its own parent. Where then
is the past? Why,
check out the horizon,
once the future, and work

in the problem. Avoid
simplistic causality:
use patchwork, collage,
co-ordinates and

(of course) parataxis.
Cat's cradle of dis-
continuous traces,
memory is

to cherish, it is
past's future.
Linear narrative
implies consolation:

it explains; to explain
is to justify.
The memories
we forget we forget

matter as much
as those we remember.
Strip off the mask,
the face underneath

is no different. Grand
recoveries often
spell cover-up, spin,
good enough to

invoke 'once upon...'
Better by far
to trust what are said
to be unimportant

memories, for
memory (sometimes)
redeems time past from
utter destruction.

We recreate time
in writing, as painters
recreate space.
In painting I hear

a harmony, silent
as the great Watteaus
and Poussin's 'A Dance
to the Music of Time',

ultrasound seen in
the Wallace Collection.
Then, without speaking,
I walk round the corner

and there in the Wigmore
Hall I await
(blotting out paintings)
whatever music,

for this in which
it tells us is
itself before it
speaks to our condition.

2008

VI   Proses

THE SECOND OLDEST POET

(For Lawrence Fixel)

It was an ordinary city. Presence and absence, for example, held sway over and within individual lives. The second oldest poet in the city was taking his afternoon stroll. He would reach the coffee house at 5.30pm as usual, the hour of the informal gathering of friends, one of the community of writers and readers of poetry that gathered every evening in the ordinary city. The only theme that all these groups had in common (apart from commitment to their art) was: the oldest poet in the city. He was the pathfinder, the wanderer leading the straggling columns of people along the way which is life. He was the king, the divine king, the One: his name was One. His powers were at their height. Or were they? As the second oldest poet sat down, he had a premonition of catastrophe, with its diametrically opposed mitigation. He ordered lemon tea and a piece of apple cake. Within half an hours, eight friends had arrived. And then a ninth rushed up: "He is dead. He is dead". No one needed to be told who was dead. In the next hour twenty six more people arrived at the coffee house. A great silence pervaded. The former second oldest poet was now the father, the king, the oldest poet in the city. This in which there is no greater fear, no greater hope.

1984 or 1985

TEXT FOR JANE BUSTIN

What could be less verbal than a Jane Bustin painting?

What could be more verbal than a Mallarmé poem?

'One does not write with ideas but with words', Mallarmé said to Degas, who fancied himself as a poet and had plenty of ideas.

As Borges might have said, we would expect the first livre d'artiste to have been created by Mallarmé (as translator) and Manet: Poe's 'Raven', and we would be right.

Let me rephrase my first sentence: not what could be less verbal but what could be more silent than a Jane Bustin painting? After all, Debussy's 'La Mer' is as wordless as a Bustin painting. Silent it is not.

(Debussy set one of Mallarmé's most significant poems, 'L'Après-midi d'un faune', to music. Mallarmé told Degas: 'I thought I had already set it to music').

My answer to the question posed above – what could be more silent than a Jane Bustin painting? – is a dead child whose absence his poet father commemorates, that 'absence [which] is condensed presence' (the phrase is from a letter of Emily Dickinson, a poet to read 'against' Mallarmé).

The dead child is Anatole Mallarmé, whom Jane Bustin too commemorates and whose existence breathes into, inspires, Bustin's paintings, via the father's heart-rending posthumously published poem.

It is neither paradoxical nor ironic that Jane Bustin depends so heavily on words during the gestation of her work exhibited at Test-Tube. Goya went further: he included words inside the visual image.

Mallarmé would have reacted to these paintings with silence. He was always eloquent.

2012

VILHELM HAMMERSHØI

(Royal Academy, London, August 2008 and in Copenhagen)

No one could accuse Hammershøi of being upbeat. And yet the light seen coming through the windows in certain interiors is the equivalent of a smile. And the doors are usually open. The artist, or the picture, is never going to laugh, but if you are a gloomy Dane, a hard won smile is something. On a good day, you might agree to design the sets for *Hedda Gabler*.

For Hammershøi, work keeps the soul's night at bay, obviating angst. His melancholy, however, has no truck with the Nordic symbolism of his time. Never pushed to total abstraction, the understated Whistler-influenced tonalities work their obsessional magic and draw us in, between the lines – those traces of architectonic primacy.

The peculiar intimacy and restraint of his work has affinities with that of Mondrian and, even more so, of Morandi. The artist's compositional template has the great Dutch masters written all over it – thus the use of a second room beyond the first – save that, lacking "human" interest, there is an uncanny feel to the intensely imagined interiors, as if Atget had photographed them.

The nearest we get to a self-portrait is in one of the interiors: an easel – and no painting standing on the easel. Metonymy suits this self-effacing master. I prefer the total interiors without the (exclusively female) figures. These figures either distract the viewer or invite unintended meanings. They are no more (but no less) important than the humanoid stove in 'The White Door'.

The life of the pictures does not depend on these figures. The viewer does not speculate about what is going on in their minds. There is no story independent of the artist's compelling vision. The unpeopled interiors allow one to colonise the space with psychic projections as one does in the empty rooms of the inspired Edgar Allan Poe Museum in Philadelphia.

One projects a structure of one's mind onto the pictures, a structure cognate with the painter's north European darkness of the soul, a darkness almost unredeemed by Mediterranean lightness of being. I say "almost" because I remember the light smiling in a handful of the pictures. This too is life.

How strange it is, how uncanny, that a picture called 'Street in London' should be of the street by the side of the British Museum where I always park my car during an evening visit there. Perhaps this phenomenon should be called a back projection. Hammershøi stayed in that street when he visited London. The British Museum symbolises nothing.

What or why does it matter that he painted these pictures? It matters because he paid attention. He paid attention to his interior landscapes because had he not done so, he would have had no way to go on living. A painting is art's way of preparing for the next painting. It is life's way of preparing for the next phase of life: to continue, to survive, until this becomes impossible, for whatever reason.

NOTEBOOK

I

1

Long ago, during my first year as an undergraduate, my father told me that a friend of his, a senior academic, made all his research notes on index cards, which were duly filed away. I remembered this when I began writing poems. Unlike my friends, who wrote poems and prose and quotes into notebooks, I never did. Everything ended up on cards or, more often, scraps of paper. I have hundreds, perhaps thousands, of these, going back fifty years.

2

From time to time I made attempts to start a notebook. Somewhere in a cupboard are the abandoned beginnings of many such aborted notebooks. The problem was that I had introjected a different work method: this may have suited a scholar accumulating and processing certain kinds of data, but it did not suit me.

3

Richard Holmes, in his book about writing biography, *Footsteps*, tells us he wrote about Shelley on the right hand pages of a notebook and himself on the left hand. That's the way to do it, as Mr Punch says. I seem to need not only the chaos every writer has swirling around his or her mind but additional chaos, you could say meta-chaos: confetti with words on. Why?

II

1

The practice feels like a mutation of bohemian nonsense concerning order which I picked up somewhere; it was a childish rebellion against organisation, which I experienced as grownup imposition. Oh dear, the time I wasted, and to a lesser extent still waste, working without notebooks, leaving bits and pieces lying around, then trying to find them and make sense of the scraps.

2

Not that a filled notebook itself is not chaotic. That indeed is one of its purposes. But it always seemed to close options, because it was finite. Index cards or scraps of paper are endless, they keep the options open. Word processors have changed everything and nothing: even on the computer, my files are poorly sorted and labelled, giving me similar problems to those I face with my scraps of paper.

3

So to repeat my earlier question, why do I make things more difficult for myself than they already are? I believe it has something to do with my academic failure which was, mainly, self-induced. I always made life more complicated than it needed to be. The academic failure involved an inability to accept reality: I did not have the mindset (even if I had the brains) to get a first class degree. I was surrounded by friends who did have the mindset. I was self-pitying and attention seeking: if I cannot be first, I will be last. I duly got an 'ordinary degree', i.e. non-honours, having changed subjects after my first year.

III

1

After graduating I had no choice but to find myself a day job outside the university, whereas virtually all my friends went off to get PhDs and teach, eventually retiring as Professors and heads of departments. Half a century later, after subsidising my life as a writer with day jobs of no interest to me, which topped up my insufficient income derived from translating and similar activities, I look back with mixed feelings.

2

Mixed feelings: despite wasting an inordinate amount of time thanks to the flaws of character or givens of temperament hinted at earlier, I have written a number of books, in addition to editing or translating others. Once in a while, even in the bad old days, everything lined up and I gave myself permission to switch on the green light. I travelled in the direction of my fear (Berryman phrase modified), wrote something down and closed that particular option.

3

There is no going back, no replay. I will never know what would have happened had I been more disciplined, more ordered. I believe there would have been more green lights. The good news is that in recent years there have been, for I have spent and spend many hours in the studio of a painter who, perhaps without knowing it, has improved my attitude.

IV

1

This painter masters chaos and disorder by application of technique and skill in the interests of story: story is how she orders her inner world, a place of fear and dread. Little by little, I came to understand that I had spent more time in defeat and creative darkness than I needed to, than is already built into the process.

2

'Do another picture', says the painter's grand-daughter, if something goes wrong. (Do another picture anyway). 'Don't throw good paint after bad', says one of her friends. Now I know that to keep all the options open is a recipe for disaster, a kind of promiscuity, a failure to commit. It is a defence against mortality, a denial of mortality. It is a decision to remain a child. However childlike, the true artist is never childish. Mozart is not Don Giovanni.

3

Leporello-like, I have a list, in my case a list of projects. I know what I want to do in future years. Fingers crossed that my health and spirit and morale stand up to the ravages of time. Slowly but surely, the list is getting shorter. With luck, I am unlearning the comfortable role of an eternally melancholy juggler in a painting by Watteau.

July 2013 (revised January 2015)

A COHERENT DEFORMATION:
ARTURO DI STEFANO

For me, although not for him, Arturo Di Stefano has been a painter-in-waiting ever since I came across his work for the first time, at his 1994 Purdy Hicks show. A verbal response has been a long time coming. Paintings, all works of art, are very patient. On the one hand, that is their job, and a necessary condition of their survival. On the other hand, they would suffer a nervous breakdown if they hung around on the off-chance that the pulses, bones and marrow of a poet who loves painting and music precisely because they are not verbal, would send the necessary signals to the mind's eye whence come the words. Yes, pulse, bone and marrow are the ante-chambers of the word. The reasons for my delay are unimportant, even to me. But now I sense the day has come:

I want to know and share with Arturo what grabs me in his work. The painterly skill, the architectonic ability, the expressive power, are right there "in your face". They could be described and perhaps even explained. But what most interests me – a poet and writer not an art critic – in his work is that the story which is the driving force of his art, generated from emotion and intellection, makes its presence felt off stage, a presence which is an absence. The implosive energy remains: the energy of the unseen destiny of anonymous persons. There is a dignity to this deliberate "back-staging" of what, in certain pictures, I read as suffering, sometimes associated with cruelty. I am not reading the process of back-staging into the paintings. I am reading it out of them. Arturo is not repressing his feelings or his thoughts. On the contrary, he is a man of great feeling and powerful intellect who deploys what painters know better than anyone how to recognise, explore and convey – surface structures of the phenomenal world as represented by documentary imagination – to tell us something of what is really going on, were we troubled enough to find out, before our very eyes. He, like William Burroughs' paranoiac, is in possession of the facts.

The artist has made a choice. One reason for refusing the option of absorption into an explicit story is to avoid the danger of frisson. I should make clear that it is possible to tell an explicit story and avoid frisson, for example in Paula Rego's 'War' and the 'Interrogator's Garden'. But that is not Arturo's way. He too directs the viewer but he trusts us in a different way – by proposing that we enter into the spirit, into the human province of the work, by generating our own story, a peopled landscape. Representation is always metamorphosis. 'Adit' and 'Aditum', to me, hint at a scary story, a back story, perhaps a cruelty being perpetrated on an innocent. Frisson is disabled.

Even without the issue of frisson, Arturo's non figurative paintings are always suggestive of human presence and he has his reasons: thus the 'chapel in Greenwich' proposes spirituality as it rises towards and at the same time draws on a distant light which creates reflection, in both senses. His 'Santo Spirito' in Florence speaks of utter holiness, protected by a plain wall. The cloisters at 'Santa Croce' cannot by any stretch of the imagination be said to be realistic, still less naturalistic. In the best sense the picture has designs upon us, indeed *is* a design upon us. The image is haunted not only by monks who are somewhere else today, at prayer or doing charitable work, but also by generations of monks who walked there. This painting, like many others by Arturo, is a homage to the lost world of the Italian ancestors of the Huddersfield-born artist. Sancta simplicitas is not possible for Arturo, but he respects and loves it, and he reminds us of Morandi, surely one of his exemplars.

Di Stefano is a remembrancer, very knowing, very modern. He directs us away from nostalgia and sentimentality by not drawing (our attention to) human beings, but requiring our inner eye to paint the persons living in that great cathedral which is the collective unconscious, the dead persons he wishes to honour, just as he honours us by requiring our collaboration. Arturo's 'Arcades' are cloisters under another name. I see Morandi's sisters quietly walking along, while, a few miles away, their brother proleptically announces Arturo di Stefano. In Arturo's 'Coram's Fields', the foundlings survive, ever lost to the parents, ever remembered.

'The Ritz' in London has not been seen, let alone represented, in this way before. The painter is not denying the man who hands out the *Evening Standard* there, let alone the billionaire entering the hotel. On the contrary, they are raised, in absentia, to their common humanity, equal in the eyes of the God who intoxicates Arturo (as he did Spinoza), even if God's presence is equated with or associated with the collective unconscious or group memory. This painting, like all Arturo's paintings, indeed like all true paintings, is an emanation of the artist's style "which is the universal sign of a 'coherent deformation'", in the phrase of Merleau-Ponty, who is citing Malraux.

One coherent deformation is Arturo's most recent work 'Painting in Raking Light'. In his studio, I looked at the two embracing figures contained in a classic Di Stefano framework and said: "Kitaj". Arturo replied: "Giotto, Joachim and Anna". Yes, Arturo's picture consciously references Giotto, but I am not wrong: it also references Kitaj, who painted works after Giotto and knew 'Joachim and Anna' very well. Giotto, Kitaj, Di Stefano: even as they make art out of life, they make art out of art. There is no contradiction: art and life give each other meaning and this is the dialectic of the imagination, which keeps us human.

2014

SCREEN MEMORY

Haidee Becker's flower paintings, not least the one I have in my sights, always disturb what Duchamp called dismissively 'the retinal aspect'. There is more to her imbricated pattern making than meets the already enchanted eye: her lifes are not so 'still', her natures not so 'mortes'.

This painting is an open book flaunting a secret. The pale blue book on the table proposes a story, which is unfolding behind the scene, symbolically confirmed by the unsmiling formal screen serving as backdrop or back cloth. The flowers seem to be or perhaps are embroidered on the screen; a screen memory.

The adjacent book does not contain the secret, it participates in the secret. The solid jug, the plain book, the equally plain table surface, foreground and stabilise the troubled quivery screen and flowers, giving us a perspective for meditation on the story.

Becker's flower paintings subvert their own decorative aspects thanks to an ominous inwardness, a painterly walk on the shadow side. She does not only make designs, her work *has* designs on the viewer who is, as it were, an intraviewer. She employs absence as a trope.

The flowers allude to a hurt in the psyche, in the soul of all who live life to the full. These flowers are a synechdoche for death, such as Gertrude uses in her famous speech to Ophelia. In the present work, this is not the death of the body, but a kind of spiritual death.

In a far recess of evening, a woman has been mourning the end of love, itself perhaps a dream in the first place; the invisible time of the flowers is an aboriginal song-line of love, a dream of love which the woman will survive when she emerges at the end of her journey, after a long winter, as charted in Schubert's *Winterreise*.

For the dream had been well and truly lived: in work and thought, in love and sex, in poetry and music – until her mad lover, a holy fool, went off the rails, at South Station in Budapest or Atocha station in Madrid. Yes, story there has been, indeed is. Haidee Becker knows something. And when you know something, you know something else.

YVES BONNEFOY:
THE RE-INVENTION OF DEATH (ONE)

Everything in his life became him like the leaving of it.

JERZYK:
THE REINVENTION OF DEATH (TWO)

Once there was Jerzyk. Then there was no Jerzyk – save that he remained ever-present in the minds and hearts of his parents and younger sister. He will survive us all, remembered in a book, a boy who experienced the worst, and died to tell the tale.

NOTES

EUROPEAN HOURS
The invocatory structure was inspired by Yves Bonnefoy's prose
poem 'Dévotion' (see my translation in *Yves Bonnefoy Reader* volume
one) Carcanet 2017. Bonnefoy's poem in turn echoes Rimbaud's
eponymous invocatory text, written in London: one of the last of his
Illuminations.

London excluded of course, the visits to the various cities, some
of them more than once, took place between 1998 and 2016. The
texts, written from memory in 2014/2015 and revised since, are not
chronologically ordered. Thanks are due to Richard Morphet for
interesting thoughts on Géricault, Delacroix and Raymond Mason,
following a chance meeting with him and his wife Sally at the Musée
Picasso.

SECTION I

FOR ALL WE KNOW
Written three years after the six months (January-June 1966) I lived at
Flat 315 (or was it 311?), 5465 South Everett, Chicago Illinois 60615.
I write more about the third of the three friends in a forthcoming
memoir, *Journey Around my Apartment*.

RETURN TO ASHKELON
This integrated sequence has been edited from several longer poems
written at the time and is, I think or hope, my final take on two
magical visits to Ashkelon with Claude and Evelyne Vigée. A few days
before one of these two visits, Claude said: "we must wait for rain

and go to Ashkelon the next day, because after the rain interesting things are washed up on the beach". Right on cue, he telephoned me at my hotel. As we drove from Jerusalem to Ashkelon, Claude pointed to a field (or perhaps he was pointing in the general direction of Ashdod) and said "it was in this field that God gave the Philistines haemorrhoids". The proof texts are First Samuel V verse 6 and First Samuel VI verses 4 and 5. There are *midrashim* on this colourful episode.

LUCIEN STRYK

This previously unpublished poem from around 1971 is a portrait of the American Zen poet and translator who lived in London. We lost touch after a few years. I checked him out in Google in 2013 when selecting poems for this book, only to find that he had died earlier in the year. On April 7, 2014, the day I wrote this note, he would have been ninety.

SECTION 11

TWELVE FRAGMENTS

These fragments were either very short to start with, or salvaged from longer poems.

SISTER OF THE SEA

The dedicatee of this fragment, Avraham Shlonsky, was one of the great Hebrew poets of the twentieth-century and a master translator from the Russian. I wrote about him in my memoir *Silent Conversations: A Reader's Life*.

MATISSE CHAPEL, VENCE

Synagoga: a reference to the medieval personifications of Church and Synagogue, Synagoga et Ecclesia. *Synagoga* is usually blindfold as, for example, in the pair of statues at Strasbourg Cathedral.

ENGLAND

This happened in 1772. The Lord Chancellor was John Scott, later Lord Eldon.

SONG RECITAL IN A CITY CHURCH

The recital, the singer's last, was held in 1971 in a Wren church, Saint Mary at Hill, which was rebuilt after the Great Fire of London. The singer was the mezzo-soprano Naomi Gerecht. I have a rare privately recorded cassette of this recital, the only direct evidence of a wondrous voice whose owner did not continue her public career as a singer. She is now an internationally respected teacher of voice in Jerusalem.

'TOUT LECTEUR EST L'ELU D'UN LIVRE'

In section three, I imagine Cairo-born francophone poet Edmond Jabès, on a visit to Cavafy's home town, Alexandria, aged nineteen or twenty, addressing the much older poet. The title of the poem is a phrase is from *Le Livre des resemblances* by Edmond Jabès. It is not impossible that the two poets *did* meet. If so, it would almost certainly have been through a publisher of early works by Jabès, Stavros Stavrinos, who was based in Cairo and Alexandria and must have known Cavafy. Stavrinos published a collected of homages to Cavafy after the poet's death in 1933. See Steven Jaron's book, *Edmond Jabès: the Hazard of Exile*.

DUBROVNIK POEM

Minyan is the Hebrew word for quorum. Ten adult male worshippers (that is, men aged thirteen or over) comprise a quorum for congregational purposes.

EMPTY HOUSES and THE TRANSLATOR ADDRESSES BORGES

In 2013, I found 'Empty Houses', an unpublished translation of a poem by Ernesto Lopez-Parra [1895–1941] in a folder which had been unopened for about forty years. Attached to the poem was a note to myself saying I translated the Spanish original from a French version but I could not remember where I had read it. However, in 2016, I found the poem in the Borges issue of *Les Cahiers de l'Herne* (1964) in an article by Borges from 1921 entitled 'Ultraismo'. The entire text is reprinted in an article on the chronology of the Ultraismo movement by César Fernandez Moreno, translated by Antoine Travers. I dedicate the translation [and my variation on it] to the memory of the poet and translator Daniel Weissbort, my friend for nearly fifty years. Professor Evelyn Fishburn tells me that the Borges article is included in volume one (1919–1929) of his *Textos Recobrados*, Buenos Aires 1997.

SAINT-PAUL DE VENCE
The words quoted are from an early poem by Donald Davie.

CHAGALL
The last stanza alludes to an aspect of Ezra Pound's poetics.

KAFKA'S TOMB
Later it turned out to be the wrong cemetery. The word *kafka* is Czech for jackdaw.
    The epigraph is from Kafka's *Letters to Milena*.

PRAYER FOR KAFKA AND OURSELVES
The poem ends with a quotation from Psalm 118.

Z. KOTOWICZ READING BACHELARD ON A TRAIN
This poem dates from 1975. In 2016 I rewrote it, replacing the unnamed speaker by my friend Z. Kotowicz, who is the author of *Gaston Bachelard: A Philosophy of the Surreal*. In 1975, smoking was still allowed on trains. The last two lines of the poem allude to two famous books by Bachelard, whose immediately post-war Sorbonne lectures on poetics were attended by Claude Vigée while, in the same period, his lectures on history of science were attended by Yves Bonnefoy.

EMMA VAN NAME
This is my account of a wonderful eighteenth-century painting

which used to be on display at the Whitney Museum of Modern Art in New York and which I saw at an exhibition at the Victoria and Albert Museum in 1976. At the time, I understood that the identity of the painter was unknown but it turns out that he may have been Joshua Johnson (which spoils my pun a bit, as does the correct pronunciation of Emma's surname). The scale of the main prop, a goblet, is completely out of proportion to the girl, so much so that it is patently deliberate and absolutely not due to incompetence.

SECTION III

PICTURE AT AN EXHIBITION
This was called 'A View of London Bridge before the Late Alterations'. It also exists as an engraving. The engraving was made in 1758. The buildings on the bridge were demolished in 1760. The word 'half-way' is in quotes because I was 35 when I wrote this poem, so half way through the span allotted in the Bible (Psalm 90). I write this note aged 72.

INVOCATIONS FOR A WORK IN CLAY
The artist was Nathalie Watt. The exhibition was at the now defunct Boadicea Gallery in London in 1978. She was born in Tunis in 1923 and died at Auxon, France, in 2011.

PARMERDE JUNPHE 1872
A few years ago, I made a pilgrimage to room 24, the garret in the legendary Hôtel Stella, 41 rue Monsieur-le-Prince (adjacent to the Polydor restaurant, whose customers have included Gide and Joyce), where Rimbaud stayed. At least, this is the room Graham Robb plumps for in his superb biography of Rimbaud, with more details supplied in a private email. Rimbaud's magnificent letter itself, with the joke date, was written from the Hôtel de Cluny, rue Victor-Cousin, by the Sorbonne, which he moved to in June 1872. You

can still stay in these hotels. A night in room 24 costs 70 euros. For Rimbaud's magnificent letter, see Pléiade editions of Rimbaud. For a translation, see *I Promise to be Good: the Letters of Arthur Rimbaud*, edited and translated by Wyatt Mason.

PROCESS VERBAL
The quote from Niedecker can be found on page 197 in her *Collected Works*, edited by Jenny Penberthy.

READING STEVENS IN HOSPITAL
The epigraph is taken from a poem whose title is embedded in my poem.

VASKO POPA
The wolf is central to many cultures and mythologies, but none more so than Serbia's.

IN MEMORIAM
'Noem' was how Michael Hamburger translated Celan's neologism 'Genicht', in order to convey Celan's rhyme: 'Mein-/gedicht, das Genicht' = 'poem, the noem' – from a 1967 poem, 'Weggebeizt' ('Etched away' or 'Bitten away'). Jeremy Adler (private communication) writes that "Celan plays on 'Genick' = back of the neck = place where Gestapo shot their victims: the word is 'Genick-Schuss'. 'Genicht' evokes 'geht nicht', i.e. "doesn't work", and the archaic verb 'ichten' is also invoked: 'To exist'. Celan recalls similar vocabulary in August Stramm: 'Ich / Wahnnichtig / Icht!'"

ET IN ARCADIA EGO
'... four minutes': allusion to the (1981) setting of the Doomsday Clock of the Bulletin of American Scientists. It is currently set at two and a half minutes to midnight... 'Four minutes' also alludes to the famous four-minute warning of a nuclear attack.

POEM-EM

The poem was inspired by the work of Michael Michaeledes and published on the occasion of his exhibition at Annely Juda Fine Art, March 1989. He died in 2015.

SECTION IV

BONNARD: THE LAST PICTURE
'Almond's trunk' = Mandelshtam in German.

BRANCA'S VINEYARD
I note, years after writing the poem, a reversal of and association with F.T. Prince's '....the dream sleeps in the stone...' from 'The Old Age of Michelangelo'.

'THE BREAD OF FAITHFUL SPEECH'
The title of this poem is taken from the last line of 'Notes towards a Supreme Fiction' by Wallace Stevens. The sub-title will remind readers of 'Thirteen Ways of Looking at a Blackbird', another poem by Stevens. For more on Pierre Rouve, some readers may want to check out my *Independent* obit of 17 December 1998.

'DAMASIO ABSTRACTED'
This was written after reading three books by the Portuguese writer, Antonio Damasio: *Descartes' Error*, *The Feeling of What Happens* and *Looking for Spinoza*. There is a later book: *Self Comes to Mind*.

UNTER DEN LINDEN
This poem explicitly intertextualises 'This Limetree Bower my Prison'. The quoted words are taken from Coleridge's great poem which, among other things, is about friendship.

PILLAR BOX

Amalia: Amalia Rodrigues, the greatest Fado singer. Eça de Queirós: Portugal's major nineteenth-century novelist.

SECTION V

ZIGZAG

'The past is cities from a train': Robert Lowell. This quote is direct. The poem alludes to many texts. See note in my book *Zigzag*.

SECTION VI

TEXT FOR JANE BUSTIN

Mallarmé's *Pour un tombeau d'Anatole* has been translated by Paul Auster under the title *A Tomb for Anatole* and by Patrick McGuiness, *For Anatole's Tomb*.

A COHERENT DEFORMATION

This text is slightly revised from the one written for Arturo Di Stefano's exhibition (catalogue), at Lemon Tree Gallery, Truro, in 2014. The title of the text, which comes from the Maurice Merleau-Ponty quote (*Signes*, 1964, page 68), is itself quoted by Merleau-Ponty from André Malraux.

SCREEN MEMORY

This text was written for Haidee Becker's exhibition (catalogue), at Patrick Bourne Gallery in 2015.

YVES BONNEFOY: THE REINVENTION OF DEATH

The sub-title alludes to Rimbaud's 're-invention of love' (in *Une Saison en enfer*). The present text is the ninth and final section of my homage to Yves Bonnefoy. An extract from my homage was published on the University of Chicago and Seagull Books websites among other tributes to Bonnefoy.

JERZYK: THE REINVENTION OF DEATH
Jerzy Feliks Urman (Jerzyk) was my second cousin once removed. He took his own life in tragic circumstances in World War Two. See my book *Jerzyk* (2016, Shearsman Books).

Appendix

This discursive text does not belong in section VI of this book, but I like it enough to reprint it after its appearance in an anthology.

OLD WYLDES

1

Old Wyldes is a former farmhouse on the southwest border of Hampstead Garden Suburb, close to the Old Bull and Bush and the phantom tube station (North End) whose unfinished platform is still visible between Hampstead and Golders Green on the Northern Line. I grew up round there and have often walked with friends to see the house before or after tea at Golders Hill Park across the road.

William Blake regularly visited his friend John Linnell at Old Wyldes, staying over on at least one occasion, according to the blue plaque on the house, which is still a private residence. In 1837, ten years after Blake's death, Dickens and his wife rented the house for a few weeks, while recovering from the death of Mary Hogarth, the novelist's sister-in-law and a key woman in his life. Dickens was working on *Oliver Twist* during this period, and it was published the following year. Bill Sikes will show up in this part of Hampstead, on the run after murdering Nancy. Surely Dickens walked around here during that fortnight and recycled a specific memory, not the less imagined for that: *Traversing the hollow by the Vale of Health, he mounted the opposite bank, and crossing the road which joins the villages of Hampstead and Highgate, made along the remaining portion of the heath to the fields at North End, in one of which he laid himself down under a hedge, and slept.*

2

My father's oldest friend Philip Lewis and his wife Lily gave me a complete set of Dickens for my barmitzvah in 1955. The books came from Boots (in those days a library and bookshop as well as a chemist's) in Piccadilly Circus or Regent Street: I knew this because one volume was missing and I went to collect it. Some years later, I realised my presents had been orchestrated by my father, since people would not have known to give me books. However, I did receive three fountain pens: 'Today I am a fountain pen,' in the words of the old joke about the barmitzvah boy's party speech. Fagin and Riah: did they too have a barmitzvah? (How many children had Lady Macbeth?) The characters from *Oliver Twist* and *Our Mutual Friend* fit perfectly this extract from Dostoevsky's interview with Dickens, even though it has now been authoritatively unmasked as a forgery: *There were two people in him, he told me: one who feels as he ought to feel and one who feels the opposite. From the one who feels the opposite I make my evil characters, from the one who feels as a man ought to feel I try to live my life. Only two people? I asked.*

3

Literary associations with Dickens are legion:
Item:
Dickens and Balzac both influenced Dostoevsky.
Item:
Evelyn Waugh's childhood house is about two hundred yards from Old Wyldes: 145 North End Road, Golders Green, NW11. Waugh would walk up the hill to post his letters in NW3. Waugh's father was a partner in Chapman and Hall, which published Dickens and Evelyn himself.

Item:

Kafka's *Metamorphosis* – Paula Rego painted me as the cockroach – parodies Dickens.

Item:

Melville's *Bartleby*, according to Borges, foreshadows Kafka and recapitulates Dickens.

Item:

Poe's famous bird, originally a parrot, was inspired by the raven in *Barnaby Rudge*. Reversed, the first two syllables of 'Nevermore' echo 'raven'.

Item:

Rabbi Lionel Blue's dog was called Riah.

Item:

Elizabeth Barrett Browning compared Balzac and Dickens as both reaching out hands to help suffering humanity, but in the case of Dickens they are *clean* hands.

4

As a student of French and Russian literature, I've read more novels by Dostoevsky and Balzac than by Dickens. That's not difficult, especially in the case of Balzac, who wrote nearly a hundred in thirty years. Dickens read, wrote and spoke French quite well. His first biographer Forster records him as saying he read Balzac. Balzac's biographer, Graham Robb, is fairly sure the English novelist did not read the French master. Bernard Berenson was sure that Eugène Sue and Victor Hugo influenced *Our Mutual Friend*.

I'm now over seventy: shall I find the time to read the Dickens novels I've not yet read? If so, what will become of my project to reread Dostoevsky? There is no time to lose.

NOTE: See *TLS* 10 April 2013 for a persuasive article by Eric Naiman proving that the interview, which fooled the scholars never mind a generalist like me, is a forgery. And yet the quote from it (in section

two of my text) is an example of *ben trovato*. The forger knew his
Dickens and his Dostoevsky.

Acknowledgments

I acknowledge magazines and other publications in which poems first appeared: *Carcanet*, Daedalus Poemcards, *Tribune, Outposts, Stand, PN Review, Modern Painters, Jane Joseph Folio*, Julia Farrer *Mandorla* etching folio, 2006, *Jewish Quarterly, European Judaism, New Humanist, Books Abroad, Holy Beggars Gazette, Platform, Scotsman, Wheels, Words Broadsheet, Words Etc, Literary Review, Transatlantic Review*, Michael Michaeledes catalogue 1989, *Journals of Pierre Menard*, MenCards, *Engraved in Flesh* (book on Piotr Rawicz), *Tree, Jerusalem Review, Israel Magazine, Los Cards*, David Gryn website, *Brooklyn Rail*, Seagull Books Catalogue and Website, Tony Frazer celebration Website, *Broadsheet* (New Zealand), Haidee Becker catalogue, Arturo Di Stefano catalogue, *A Sociology of Educating*

ANTHOLOGIES
Epitaphs for Lorine, 1973
For John Riley, 1979
Poetry Dimension 8, 1980
Voices in the Ark, 1980
Homage to Mandelstam, 1981
The Full Note: Lorine Niedecker, 1983
The Poetry of Solitude: a Tribute to Edward Hopper, 1995
Eddie's Own Acquarius, 2005
All that Mighty Heart: London Poems, 2008
This Line is Not for Turning, 2011
Soul Feathers, 2011
A Mutual Friend, 2012

Paula (privately published), 2014
The Arts of Peace, 2014
Poems for Regina Derieva, 2015

The poems date from 1964 to 2015. Some are reprinted (unchanged or revised) from earlier books: *The Same River Twice* (Carcanet 1976), *After the Dream* (Cauldron Press, USA, 1980) and *Zigzag* (Carcanet/ Northern House 2011).

For a detailed publishing history and account of revisions of the two long poems in section V, 'Zigzag' and 'Mandorla', see the notes in my book *Zigzag*.

About a third of the poems in this book are previously unpublished.

Apart from the prologue, 'European Hours', the order of the poems and proses is broadly chronological.

Over the years, some poems were translated into French, Russian, Hebrew, Serbo-Croat, Macedonian, Mongolian, Turkish, Spanish, Slovenian and Chinese: my thanks to the translators and periodicals and anthologies concerned.

I am grateful to Helen Tookey for her care and attention. Thanks too to Deryn Rees-Jones, Vesna Main and Paula Rego for their comments at different stages.

Index of Titles

6.30 p.m. On the Dot   35

Against Anxiety   68
Amsterdam   59
Ancient Beams   72
Ancient of Days   67
Antique Land   87
Architexture   99
Autumnal   71

Balthus   56
Beach   21
Blackheath: Autumn   20
Bonnard: the Last Picture   90
Branca's Vineyard   93
'The Bread of Faithful Speech'   94
Breughel to Auden   82

Careless Love   42
Catalogue Sonnet   75
Chagall   55
Checkpoint Charlie   34
Chez Maeght (Saint-Paul de Vence)   54
Childhood   19
Circle of Knowledge   98
A Coherent Deformation: Arturo Di Stefano   142
Colombine at the Picasso Exhibition, Paris, November 1996 92

'Damasio Abstracted'   102
Dimension   20

Dream Time   51
Dubrovnik Poem   47
Dunedin: Botanical Gardens   107

Early Photograph of Michael Hamburger   39
East Sixth Street, 1966   16
Edward Hopper   61
Emma Van Name   64
Empty Houses   50
England   43
Et in Arcadia Ego   79
European Hours   3
Evening of the Rose   33

Final Proof   103
For All We Know   22
Found Poem   105
Fran Sinclair   89

Grandmother   40
The Grave   12

Halfway through Life   73
Headland   81
Heater   15
A History of Silence   60

In his Death   58
In Memoriam [Veronica Forrest-Thomson]   41
In Memoriam [Nadezhda Yakovlevna Mandelshtam]   78
In Memoriam Gisèle Celan-Lestrange   91
Invisible Ink   29
Invocations for a Work in Clay   71

Jerzyk: The Reinvention of Death (Two)   146
Joseph Rudolf, 92, Speaks to his Grandson   41

Kafka's Tomb   58
Kensington Palace Gardens   52

Land of Ancient Moons   14
Last Poem of Karl Kraus (1936)   64
Late Night   43
The Lost Tribe   42
Lucien Stryk   32

Mandorla   113
Manifold Circle   28
Matisse Chapel, Vence   42
Mother Tongue   40

Necessary Fiction   16
Noonday   80
Notebook   139

Obsession: A Structure   13
Old Man   76
Old Wyldes   159
Onion   40

Parmerde Junphe 1872   74
Pebble   30
Picture at an Exhibition   70
Picture on the Wall: No-Man's-Landscape   31
Pillar Box, Well Walk NW3   110
Poem-em   82
Power Cut   57
Prayer for Kafka and Ourselves   59
A Presence   49
Primrose Gardens, London NW3   39
Process Verbal   77

Reading Stevens in Hospital   77
Recollection   41
Redemption Song   63
The Reflection   25
Removal Man   97
Return to Ashkelon   26
Reveille   47
Rider on the Rocking Horse   101

Saint-Paul de Vence 53
The Same River Twice 62
Screen Memory 145
The Second Oldest Poet 135
Sister of the Sea 39
Song Recital in a City Church 45
Stones 11
Structure of Feeling 24
The Sound of the Land: Reflection 17

Text for Jane Bustin 136
Three Poems of the Grave 57
To a Voice 21
'Tout lecteur est l'élu d'un livre' 45
The Translator Addresses Borges 50
Tree 11
'The True Inflections...' 69
Twelve Fragments 39
Two Linked Poems for Charlie 107

Unter den Linden 104

Vasko Popa in Cambridge 78
Vilhelm Hammershøi 137

The Waves 12
Wellington: Queen's Wharf 108

You, Painting 88
Your Mind Surprises Itself 109
Yves Bonnefoy: The Re-invention of Death (One) 146

Z. Kotowicz Reading Bachelard on a Train 62
Zigzag (Teaching Autobiography, 2000–2003) 119

Index of First Lines

A presence tinges my remembering   31
A voice across the air   94
Absence all around the common   20
Again   87
'Always the Jew was treated   47
Apparent perfection is   28
At the time I knew I'd lost it   105

Before the entrance is the pleasure-   54
Between sign   63

Cross the lines of a life   40

Death is a circle reduced   89
Don't ask what I've been doing all the time   64
Down Grey Street, and Dean Street   43

Each waits for the other to come near   24
Early afternoon, back end of summer   107
Edging the meridian   80
Emma, what is in a name?   64
'Emperor priest'   78
Everything in his life   146

Flying west has dislocated me   98
For me, although not for him   142
Found in the distances of childhood   39
Freeing the line it makes   113
From the window   90

Haidee Becker's flower paintings   145
Half-awake   62
Here, late at night, the ground floor window   59
He smiles: the interview is over   40
He took my words   62
His ancient moments dropped like leaves   11
His virgins meditate, they stare into   56
Horizon   55
How shall I know for certain there is no past   74

I am determined by my class   75
I ask my friend to visit Kafka's grave   58
I dismember the lines of your beautiful poem   43
I disturb them, to be reassured   11
I feel an urge to cross the water   108
I hear them knocking   40
I leave your flat, you know   110
I live on the edge, on edge   20
I loved the man   45
I make a move   97
I put my book on the table   34
I read each phrase, each line, re-read   77
I said things   60
I stand before an Auerbach picture   69
I walk across the park   52
I write   57
'If you interrupt me once more I   41
Imagine dead   79
In a dark time   78
In his death   58
In the East End   103
It was an ordinary city   135

Leaving my study   49
Let the exiles in-gather   33
Long ago, during my first year   139

Mind is dancing   109
Mother of lightning   71
My mind is made up of images   102

My son, my daughter 81

No one could accuse Hammershøi 137
Not 25
Now all I have is the presence 21

Objectivists are metaphysical 61
Old man 76
Old Wyldes is a former farmhouse 159
Once by the lake in Chicago I recalled 41
Once in the valley of Jezreel 39
Once more I name a city 53
Once there was Jerzyk 146
One softly hinted 22
Our daily work is touched by 82

Pebble, 'magic mountain', packed 30

Rise and shine 47

She died before her time: is named the late 41
She leaves me at the photographs 92
Sun sets the scene of quiet *without*: the land 71
Synagoga, weep for joy 42

Ten seconds later 35
The hardened heart of rock was still 16
The house is full of absence 50
The river is the mother of the city 70
The sleeping passion of volcanic stone 93
The song of a Jewess returns us 45
The street was whole 19
They sweep away pebbles 12
Through myself, I see 17
Through the train 51
To die old 67
To sense 77
Towards the focal point 15
Truly, a philosopher 32

Uninvited	13
Upstairs lived	101
Walking around the room	99
Walking blindly	21
We are the little people	42
We have lost our voices	29
We move house tomorrow	39
We pass the orange-groves	26
We walk alone on our roots	59
Weather-beaten	12
Well, they are gone, and here must I remain	104
What could be less verbal	136
What is it about you	72
Where we find ourselves	119
Write the history	68
Yellow with pears, and full	73
You landed on the moon this afternoon	42
You, painting	88
Your pictures speak to me, but not to you	16
Your presence overflows	50
Your reliefs	82
Your stillness brings back memories of stone	14
Zhivago	91